SHIʿI INTERPRETATIONS OF ISLAM

The Institute of Ismaili Studies

Ismaili Texts and Translations Series, 13

Previously published titles:

1. Ibn al-Haytham. *The Advent of the Fatimids: A Contemporary Shiʿi Witness.* An edition and English translation of Ibn al-Haytham's *Kitāb al-munāẓarāt*, by Wilferd Madelung and Paul E. Walker (2000).
2. Muḥammad b. ʿAbd al-Karīm al-Shahrastānī. *Struggling with the Philosopher: A Refutation of Avicenna's Metaphysics.* A new Arabic edition and English translation of al-Shahrastānī's *Kitāb al-muṣāraʿa*, by Wilferd Madelung and Toby Mayer (2001).
3. Jaʿfar b. Manṣūr al-Yaman. *The Master and the Disciple: An Early Islamic Spiritual Dialogue.* Arabic edition and English translation of Jaʿfar b. Manṣūr al-Yaman's *Kitāb al-ʿālim wa'l-ghulām*, by James W. Morris (2001).
4. Idrīs ʿImād al-Dīn. *The Fatimids and their Successors in Yaman: The History of an Islamic Community.* Arabic edition and English summary of Idrīs ʿImād al-Dīn's *ʿUyūn al-akhbār*, vol. 7, by Ayman F. Sayyid, in collaboration with Paul E. Walker and Maurice A. Pomerantz (2002).
5. Naṣīr al-Dīn Ṭūsī. *Paradise of Submission: A Medieval Treatise on Ismaili Thought.* A new Persian edition and English translation of Naṣīr al-Dīn Ṭūsī's *Rawḍa-yi taslīm*, by S.J. Badakhchani with an introduction by Hermann Landolt and a philosophical commentary by Christian Jambet (2005).
6. al-Qāḍī al-Nuʿmān. *Founding the Fatimid State: The Rise of an Early Islamic Empire.* An annotated English translation of al-Qāḍī al-Nuʿmān's *Iftitāḥ al-daʿ*wa, by Hamid Haji (2006).
7. Idrīs ʿImād al-Dīn. *ʿUyūn al-akhbār wa-funūn al-āthār.* Arabic critical edition in 7 volumes by Ahmad Chleilat, Mahmoud Fakhoury, Yousef S. Fattoum, Muhammad Kamal, Ma'moun al-Sagherji and Ayman F. Sayyid (2007–2010).

8. Aḥmad b. Ibrāhīm al-Naysābūrī. *Degrees of Excellence: A Fatimid Treatise on Leadership in Islam.* A New Arabic Edition and English translation of Aḥmad b. Ibrāhīm al-Naysābūrī's *Kitāb Ithbāt al-Imāma,* by Arzina R. Lalani (2010).
9. Ḥamīd al-Dīn Aḥmad b. ʿAbd Allāh al-Kirmānī. *Master of the Age: An Islamic Treatise on the Necessity of the Imamate.* A critical edition of the Arabic text and English translation of Ḥamīd al-Dīn al-Kirmānī's *al-Maṣābīḥ fī ithbāt al-imāma,* by Paul E. Walker (2007).
10. *Orations of the Fatimid Caliphs: Festival Sermons of the Ismaili Imams.* An edition of the Arabic texts and English translation of Fatimid *khuṭba*s, by Paul E. Walker (2009).
11. Taqī al-Dīn Aḥmad b. ʿAlī al-Maqrīzī. *Towards a Shiʿi Mediterranean Empire: Fatimid Egypt and the Founding of Cairo.* The reign of the Imam-caliph al-Muʿizz, from al-Maqrīzī's *Ittiʿāẓ al-ḥunafāʾ bi-akhbār al-aʾimma al-Fāṭimiyyīn al-khulafāʾ*, translated by Shainool Jiwa (2009).
12. Taqī al-Dīn Aḥmad b. ʿAlī al-Maqrīzī. *Ittiʿāẓ al-ḥunafāʾ bi-akhbār al-aʾimma al-Fāṭimiyyīn al-khulafāʾ*. Arabic critical edition in 4 volumes, with an introduction and notes by Ayman F. Sayyid (2010).

Shiʿi Interpretations of Islam

Three Treatises on Theology and Eschatology

A Persian edition and English translation of
Naṣīr al-Dīn Ṭūsī's
Tawallā wa tabarrā, *Maṭlūb al-muʾminīn*
and *Āghāz wa anjām*

by

S. J. Badakhchani

I.B.Tauris *Publishers*
LONDON • NEW YORK
in association with
The Institute of Ismaili Studies
LONDON

Published in 2010 by I.B.Tauris & Co Ltd
6 Salem Rd, London W2 4BU
175 Fifth Avenue, New York NY 10010
www.ibtauris.com

in association with The Institute of Ismaili Studies
210 Euston Road, London NW1 2DA
www.iis.ac.uk

Distributed in the United States of America and in Canada Exclusively by
Palgrave Macmillan, 175 Fifth Avenue, New York NY 10010

ISBN 978 1 84885 594 6

A full CIP record for this book is available from the British Library
A full CIP record for this book is available from the Library of Congress

Library of Congress catalog card: available

Typeset in Minion Tra for The Institute of Ismaili Studies
Printed and bound in Great Britain by TJ International Ltd, Padstow, Cornwall

Mixed Sources
Product group from well-managed forests and other controlled sources
www.fsc.org Cert no. SGS-COC-2482
© 1996 Forest Stewardship Council
FSC

The Institute of Ismaili Studies

The Institute of Ismaili Studies was established in 1977 with the object of promoting scholarship and learning on Islam, in the historical as well as contemporary contexts, and a better understanding of its relationship with other societies and faiths.

The Institute's programmes encourage a perspective which is not confined to the theological and religious heritage of Islam, but seeks to explore the relationship of religious ideas to broader dimensions of society and culture. The programmes thus encourage an interdisciplinary approach to the materials of Islamic history and thought. Particular attention is also given to issues of modernity that arise as Muslims seek to relate their heritage to the contemporary situation.

Within the Islamic tradition, the Institute's programmes promote research on those areas which have, to date, received relatively little attention from scholars. These include the intellectual and literary expressions of Shiʿism in general, and Ismailism in particular.

In the context of Islamic societies, the Institute's programmes are informed by the full range and diversity of cultures in which Islam is practised today, from the Middle East, South and Central Asia, and Africa to the industrialized societies of the West, thus taking into consideration the variety of contexts which shape the ideals, beliefs and practices of the faith.

These objectives are realized through concrete programmes and activities organized and implemented by various departments of the Institute. The Institute also collaborates periodically, on a programme-specific basis, with other institutions of learning in the United Kingdom and abroad.

The Institute's academic publications fall into a number of interrelated categories:

1. Occasional papers or essays addressing broad themes of the relationship between religion and society, with special reference to Islam.
2. Monographs exploring specific aspects of Islamic faith and culture, or the contributions of individual Muslim thinkers or writers.
3. Editions or translations of significant primary or secondary texts.
4. Translations of poetic or literary texts which illustrate the rich heritage of spiritual, devotional and symbolic expressions in Muslim history.
5. Works on Ismaili history and thought, and the relationship of the Ismailis to other traditions, communities and schools of thought in Islam.
6. Proceedings of conferences and seminars sponsored by the Institute.
7. Bibliographical works and catalogues which document manuscripts, printed texts and other source materials.

This book falls into category three listed above.

In facilitating these and other publications, the Institute's sole aim is to encourage original research and analysis of relevant issues. While every effort is made to ensure that the publications are of a high academic standard, there is naturally bound to be a diversity of views, ideas and interpretations. As such, the opinions expressed in these publications must be understood as belonging to their authors alone.

Table of Contents

Acknowledgements

It is a most rewarding task for me to voice my sincere thanks and profound sense of indebtedness to the academic staff, management and library personnel of The Institute of Ismaili Studies for their encouragement, support and assistance in the preparation of the present work. Their contribution has been invaluable, in particular when translating a text where three languages are involved and the subject matter is among the most complicated in the theological-philosophical discourse of Islam.

My task would have been impossible without the constant encouragement of Dr Farhad Daftary, Professor Wilferd Madelung's careful reading, comments and corrections of the work in its various stages of production, and the helpful advice of Professor Hermann Landolt, Professor M. A. Amir-Moezzi, Professor Azim Nanji, Dr Aziz Esmail, Dr F. M. Hunzai, M. R. Jozi, D. Mohammad Poor, and other friends and colleagues too numerous to name here—to all of whom I am forever thankful.

Special thanks are due to Kutub Kassam, who not only edited the text with great care and diligence, but also contributed significantly to the shaping of the introduction and its final presentation. I am also grateful to Nadia Holmes for her assistance in producing the final copy of the text, together with its bibliography and index.

Finally, my words of appreciation would be incomplete were I not to mention the support and inspiration that I have received from my wife, Parichehr Badakhchani, without whom this work would not have materialized.

S. J. B.

Introduction

The three short treatises introduced here are among several works on the doctrines of the early Nizārī Ismaili community of Iran produced during the 7th/13th century by the celebrated Muslim theologian, philosopher and scientist Naṣīr al-Dīn Ṭūsī. The authorship of these treatises is confirmed by Ṭūsī's name which appears in the preludes to the texts. Consequently, almost all scholars and bibliographers on his life and writings have included these texts in the inventory of Ṭūsī's works. While *Tawallā wa tabarrā* (Solidarity and Dissociation) and *Maṭlūb al-mu'minīn* (Desideratum of the Faithful) have until now remained relatively obscure for various reasons, *Āghāz wa anjām* (Origin and Destination), the last and longest of the three, is well-known in Shi'i literature. The present volume renders, for the first time, new edited versions and complete English translations of the three treatises.

The author and his works

Naṣīr al-Dīn Ṭūsī, Muḥammad b. Muḥammad b. Ḥasan was born in 597/1201 in Ṭūs in the suburbs of present-day Mashhad in Iran and died in Baghdad in 672/1274. There are a number of well documented books[1] and articles[2] on the life of Ṭūsī, including the

1. See in particular M. Taqī Mudarris-i Raḍawī, *Yādbūd-i haft ṣadumīn sāl-i Khwāja Naṣīr al-Dīn Ṭūsī* (Tehran, 1335 Sh./1956) and his *Aḥwāl wa āthār-i Abū Ja'far Muḥammad b. Muḥammad b. Ḥasan al-Ṭūsī* (2nd ed., Tehran, 1354 Sh./1975); as well as M. Mudarrisī Zanjānī, *Sargudhasht wa 'aqa'id-i falsafī-yi Khwāja Naṣīr al-Dīn Ṭūsī* (Tehran, 1335 Sh./1956).

2. Farhad Daftary, 'Nasir al-Din Tusi and the Isma'ilis', in his *Ismailis in Medieval Muslim Societies* (London, 2005), pp. 171–182; and Hamid Dabashi, 'The Philosopher/Vizier: Khwāja Naṣīr al-Dīn Ṭūsī and the Isma'ilis', in F. Daftary, ed.,

introduction to my edition of his autobiographical essay, *Sayr wa sulūk*.[3]

Ṭūsī's early childhood coincided with the rise of the Mongols as a military power in Central Asia and their advance towards the Iranian territories. His father, a Twelver Shi'i and most probably engaged in clerical activities, seems to have been a broad-minded person desiring his son to study all the sciences, in particular those related to religion, as widely and objectively as possible, and not to confine the horizon of his thought to what was available in his own surroundings. He was apparently under the influence of two famous men of letters, the philosopher Bābā Afḍal al-Dīn Kāshānī and the well-known theologian-heresiographer Muḥammad b. ʿAbd al-Karīm Shahrastānī, both of whom were inclined to the teachings of Nizārī Ismailism. In the *Sayr wa sulūk*, Ṭūsī mentions these two scholars and recounts the encouragements of his father concerning the pursuit of religious knowledge.[4] Such an intellectual milieu seems to have imbued Ṭūsī from an early age with a lifelong thirst for knowledge and helped to shape his multi-faceted scholarly personality.

In the *Sayr wa sulūk*, Ṭūsī recounts his quest for knowledge in considerable detail. Having exhausted his examination of the doctrines of all the major schools and communities of Islam without attaining satisfaction, he happened to come across a book, the *Fuṣūl-i mubārak wa muqaddas* (Blessed and Sacred Chapters), containing the sermons of the Nizārī Ismaili Imam Ḥasan ʿAlā Dhikrihi al-Salām (d. 561/1166).[5] This discovery proved to be pivotal in Ṭūsī's intellectual journey, so much so that at about the age of twenty years, he began to communicate with certain dignitaries of the Ismaili *daʿwat* (mission) and, around the year 624/1227, he joined the court of the Ismaili governor of Quhistān in eastern Iran, Nāṣir al-Dīn Muḥtashim (d.

Mediaeval Isma'ili History and Thought (Cambridge, 1996), pp. 231–245.

3. Naṣīr al-Dīn Ṭūsī, *Sayr wa sulūk* ed., and tr. S. J. Badakhchani as *Contemplation and Action: The Spiritual Autobiography of a Muslim Scholar* (London, 1998), pp. 1–19.

4. Ṭūsī, *Sayr wa sulūk*, pp. 26§6–7, 55n4 and 56n5.

5. The *Fuṣūl* has not survived, but scattered fragments of it are found in post-Alamūt Ismaili literature. Ṭūsī quotes several passages from it in his *Rawḍa-yi taslīm*, ed. and tr. S. J. Badakhchani as *Paradise of Submission: A Medieval Treatise on Ismaili Thought* (London, 2005), pp. 122–125§355–359.

655/1257), as a resident scholar at his castle. Initially, Ṭūsī appears to have dedicated his time to composing and translating works on ethics and astronomy, in addition to providing scholarly service to the governor and his associates. In both fields he proved to be a highly erudite and accomplished person, with an unrivalled mastery of a variety of subjects, which was much appreciated by the governor.

It was probably in Quhistān that Ṭūsī finally converted to the Ismaili faith and became thoroughly acquainted with its doctrines in both their exoteric and esoteric aspects. His enthusiasm for the faith, together with superior intellectual skills, paved the ground for his transfer around 633/1235 to the fortress of Alamūt in the Alburz mountains of northern Iran, the headquarters of the Nizārī Ismaili state, to continue his scholarship under the patronage of Imam ʿAlāʾ al-Dīn Muḥammad (d. 653/1255). Ṭūsī's transfer to Alamūt may have been motivated in part by its reputation as a centre of learning and scholarship, with a library and observatory where he could better pursue his scientific and literary activities. Ṭūsī may also have been motivated by the desire to be in the personal service of Imam ʿAlāʾ al-Dīn, especially for the exposition of Ismaili doctrines, including the doctrine of *qiyāma* which had been promulgated some 75 years earlier by the Imam's great-grandfather Ḥasan ʿAlā Dhikrihi al-Salām (as discussed in the following section).

The imamate of ʿAlāʾ al-Dīn coincided with a period of heightened political tension in Iran because of the ever growing threat of the Mongols. Having devastated Trans-Oxiana and Khurāsān with unprecedented cost of lives, the Mongol armies were now poised to advance into the heartlands of the Muslim world. The critical outlook was evident in the flood of refugees who poured into eastern Iran from Central Asia, including several Sunni and Shiʿi scholars who sought sanctuary in the Ismaili fortresses. It was at this time that Ṭūsī came to Alamūt and remained there for twenty years until the fortress fell to the Mongols in 654/1256.

In spite of the dangerous circumstances, this period constituted the most creative and productive period in Ṭūsī's life, during which he composed his most seminal works on philosophy and astronomy that received acclaim in both Ismaili and non-Ismaili circles. Apparently, he established a close relationship with Imam ʿAlāʾ al-Dīn, who appointed him to a senior rank in the Nizārī *daʿwat* as indicated by his honorifics of *dāʿī al-duʿāt* (chief missionary) and *khwāja-yi kāʾināt* (master of creation).[6] Among other Muslims he came to be known as *sulṭān al-muḥaqiqīn* (lord of the truth-seekers) and *ustād al-bashar* (teacher of humanity).[7]

The outcome of Ṭūsī's scholarly activities in both Quhistān and Alamūt can be grouped into three broad categories. As one may expect, he conducted regular lectures on Ismaili doctrines to member of the *daʿwat* in a manner reminiscent of the Fatimid tradition of *majālis al-ḥikma* (sessions of wisdom) firmly established by al-Qāḍī al-Nuʿmān and al-Muʾayyad fī al-Dīn al-Shīrāzī.[8] Fortunately, some of Ṭūsī's lectures delivered in Alamūt were recorded and put together by his colleague, the poet Ḥasan-i Maḥmūd-i Kātib, in the *Rawḍa-yi taslīm*.[9] Ṭūsī also embarked on writing a number of scholarly works on Ismaili thought commissioned by his patrons. Among those he produced in Quhistān, the most famous is his treatise on ethics, *Akhlāq-i Nāṣirī*,[10] followed by *Akhlāq-i Muḥtashimī*,[11] *Sayr wa sulūk*[12] and *Tawallā wa tabarrā*. In Alamūt, he worked on *Maṭlūb al-muʾminīn*, *Āghāz wa anjām*, and *Rawḍa-yi taslīm*, a treatise on free will and predestination, *Jabr wa ikhtiyār*,[13] as well as an Arabic work

6. Ṭūsī, *Rawḍa*, trans., p. 13.

7. Mudarris-i Raḍawī, *Aḥwāl wa āthār*, p. 46.

8. See Heinz Halm, 'The Ismaili Oath of Allegiance (*ʿahd*) and the 'Sessions of Wisdom' (*majālis al-ḥikma*) in Fatimid Times', in Daftary, *Mediaeval Ismaʿili History and Thought'*, pp. 91–115.

9. On the authorship of *Rawḍa*, see my Preface to the translation, pp. xv–xvi.

10. Ṭūsī, *Akhlāq-i Nāṣirī* ed. Mujtabā Mīnuwī and ʿA. R. Ḥaydarī (Tehran, 1356 Sh./1977), tr. G. M. Wickens as *The Nasirean Ethics* (London, 1964). On the Ismaili orientation of this work, see Wilferd Madelung, 'Naṣīr al-Dīn Ṭūsī's Ethics between Philosophy, Shiʿism and Sufism', in R. G. Hovannisian, ed., *Ethics in Islam* (Malibu, CA), 1985, pp. 85–101.

11. Ṭūsī, *Akhlāq-i Muḥtashimī*, ed. M. T. Dānish-pazhūh (Tehran, 1339 Sh./1960).

12. It appears that *Sayr wa sulūk* may have been revised in Alamūt or perhaps after its fall, for Ṭūsī twice uses the invocation, 'May God be pleased with him', for the Ismaili dignitary Muḥtashim Shihāb al-Dīn (pp. 30–31§14), indicating that he had already passed away, which occurred towards or after the fall of Alamūt.

13. This treatise in which Ṭūsī quotes Imām Ḥasan ʿAlā Dhikrihi al-Salām, bears different titles such as *Jabr wa qadr*, *Qaḍā wa qadar* and *Jabr wa ikhtiyār*.

entitled *al-Dustūr wa daʿwat al-muʾminīn lil-ḥuḍūr* which, although attributed to Imam ʿAlāʾ al-Dīn, came most probably from the pen of Ṭūsī.[14] There are four other Ismaili treatises attributed to Ṭūsī which are probably not by him: *Jawāb bi Kiyā Shāh Amīr* (Answers to Kiyā Shāh Amīr) on Qurʾānic hermeneutics and compiled most probably by Imam Ḥasan ʿAlā Dhikrihi al-Salām; *Nāma bi ahālī-yi Qazwīn* (Letter to the people of Qazwīn); *Majārāt-i Khwāja* (Debates of Khwāja); and *Risāla dar niʿmat-hā, khushī-hā wa ladhdhat-hā* (Treatise on Comfort, Happiness and Joyfulness).

In addition to these literary activities connected directly with Ismaili doctrines, Ṭūsī composed a number of philosophical works devoted mainly to the defence and elaboration of Ibn Sīnā's writings. Ṭūsī was a great admirer of Ibn Sīnā's synthesis of Aristotelian, Neo-Platonic and Islamic intellectual traditions, wherein he found much that was in agreement with Ismaili hermeneutical literature.[15] His masterly commentary on Ibn Sīnā's *Sharḥ al-ishārāt wa al-tanbīhāt*, in which he refutes the criticism of Fakhr al-Dīn al-Rāzī, was commenced in Quhistān and finalized in Alamūt. His treatises on Aristotelian logic, the *Asās al-iqtibās*, and on astronomy, *al-Tadhkira fī al-hayʾa*, were both undertaken in Alamūt.[16]

The fortunes of the Nizārī Ismailis suffered a devastating reversal in 654/1256 with the invasion of Persian-speaking lands by the Mongols

---

There are many copies of its manuscript in various collections in Iranian libraries and it has been published several times. Mudarris Raḍawī's edition in Ṭūsī's *Majmūʿa-yi rasāʾil* (Tehran, 1335 Sh./1956), pp. 8–27, is based on an earlier edition and a number of well-known manuscripts. For details see his introduction to the *Majmūʿa*.

14. The scribe of this treatise, Shams al-Dīn Aḥmad b. Yaʿqūb al-Ṭayyibī, records in the colophon that he had heard the text from 'the illustrious *dāʿī* Naṣīr al-Dīn'. For details see ʿĀrif Tāmir, *Arbaʿa rasāʾil Ismāʿīlīyya* (Salamiyya, Syria, 1952), p. 101.

15. This is evident, for example, in Ibn Sīnā's notion of the 'Unknowable God', which Ṭūsī renders in the *Rawḍa*-(p.16§1) and *Maṭlūb* (§4) as 'Necessary Existence' (*wājib al-wujūd*) that is altogether beyond the realm of human knowledge and comprehension.

16. Ṭūsī, *Sharḥ al-Ishārāt wa al-tanbīhāt* (Tehran, 1377/1957); *Asās al-iqtibās*, ed. M. Mudarris Raḍawī (Tehran, 1335 Sh./1976); *al-Tadhkira fī al-hayʾa*, ed. and tr. F. G. Ragep in his *Naṣīr al-Dīn Ṭūsī's Memoir on Astronomy* (New York, 1993), pp. 89–341.

under the command of the warlord Hülegü. Commencing with the destruction of Ismaili fortresses in eastern and northern Iran, the Mongol advance culminated with the bloody capture of Baghdad and termination of the Abbasid caliphate within a year from each other.[17] During the siege of Alamūt, the Ismaili Imam of the time, Rukn al-Dīn Khurshāh, who had succeeded ʿAlāʾ al-Dīn in 653/1255, sought unsuccessfully to negotiate with the Mongols. Eventually he was forced to surrender, exiled to Mongolia and subsequently murdered in mysterious circumstances.

The role of Ṭūsī in the negotiations that led to the surrender of Alamūt and his defection to the Mongols is a controversial aspect of his career about which little is known. There are diverse and sometimes contradictory reports which, for a number of reasons, cannot be relied upon, and it is unlikely that we will ever reach a firm conclusion regarding his conduct.[18] Whatever Ṭūsī's motivations, it is possible to surmise that he chose to ensure his survival by distancing himself from the Ismailis and offering his services to the conquering Mongols. This course of action not only permitted him to continue his scholarship under Mongol patronage at the Marāgha observatory constructed especially for him in Azerbaijan, but also enabled him to dissuade the invaders from a total annihilation of the Iranian cultural heritage.

Ṭūsī's scholarly work in the post-Alamūt period of his life was focused mainly on the establishment of the Marāgha observatory and compilation of its astronomical tables, the *Zīj-i Īlkhānī*. He also continued to champion Ibn Sīnā against the criticism of Fakhr al-Dīn al-Rāzī[19] and Shahrastānī.[20] His interest in theological issues remained

17. For a comprehensive study of the rise and fall of Nizari Ismaili power in Iran, see M. G. Hodgson, *The Order of Assassins: The Struggle of the Nizārī Ismāʿīlīs against the Islamic World* (The Hague, 1955); and F. Daftary, *The Ismāʿīlīs: Their History and Doctrines* (2nd revised ed., Cambridge, 2007), pp. 301–405.

18. See my Introduction to *Sayr wa sulūk* (pp. 7–8) for a discussion of this episode in Ṭūsī's life.

19. Ṭūsī's commentary entitled *Talkhīṣ al-muḥaṣṣal* was edited by A. A. Nūrānī (Tehran, 1359 Sh./1980).

20. See Ṭūsī's *Maṣāriʿ al-muṣāriʿ*, ed. Ḥasan al-Muʿizzī (Qumm, 1405/1984), which is a critique of Shahrastānī's *Kitāb al-muṣāraʿa*, ed. and tr. Wilferd Madelung and Toby Mayer as *Struggling with the Philosopher: A Refutation of Avicenna's Metaphysics* (London, 2001).

unabated, with the production of a number of works on Twelver Shiʿi theology, such as *Risālat al-imāma*[21] and *Tajrīd al-iʿtiqād*,[22] as well as a treatise on Islamic mysticism entitled *Awṣāf al-ashrāf*.[23] By the time Ṭūsī died, he is said to have composed over 150 works of varying lengths on diverse subjects which established his reputation as the leading Muslim scholar of the Mongol era.[24] By advocating Shiʿi doctrines from philosophical and mystical perspectives, including a number of Ismaili ideas which he never completely renounced, Ṭūsī was able to pave the ground for the emergence in subsequent centuries of distinctive schools of philosophical and mystical theology in Iran. In certain respects, this outcome may be regarded as a development of Ismaili doctrines which Ṭūsī had imbibed and expounded for more than two decades prior to the Mongol invasion.[25]

By the time Alamūt fell to the Mongols, Ṭūsī had already depicted the major trends in Nizārī Ismaili thought and presented them in a profoundly philosophical and hermeneutic manner in the *Rawḍa-yi taslīm*, and in a more abbreviated form in the three treatises presented here. The close relationship between these texts and the *Rawḍa* is quite apparent, as illustrated in the annotations to these texts. Their differences, apart from the subject-matter, are merely in the style of authorship and the readership for which they were intended. Whereas the *Rawḍa* is aimed at a fairly erudite membership of the Nizārī *daʿwat* well-versed in the philosophical and religious sciences of the day, the *Tawallā* and *Maṭlūb* are much shorter treatises addressed to junior

---

21. Ṭūsī, *Risālat al-imāma*, in *Talkhīṣ al-muḥaṣṣal*, pp. 424–433.

22. The *Tajrīd al-iʿtiqād* is printed with ʿAllāma Ḥillī's comments known as *Kashf al-murād*, ed. Abū al-Ḥasan Shaʿrānī (Tehran, 1398/1969).

23. Ṭūsī, *Awṣāf al-ashrāf*, ed. Māyil Harawī (Mashhad, 1361 Sh./ 1982). Nasrollah Pourjavady, in his article 'Awṣāf al-Ashrāf' in *Naṣīr al-Dīn Ṭūsī Philosophe, et savant du XIIIe siècle*, ed. N. Pourjavady and Z. Vesel (Tehran, 2000), pp. 39–40, regards this book as 'a treatise on mysticism from a philosophical point of view', whereas H. Dabashi maintains in 'The Philosopher/Vizier: Khwāja Naṣīr al-Dīn al-Ṭūsī and the Ismaʿilis', that the *Awṣāf* is an Ismaili text.

24. W. Madelung, 'Naṣīr al-Dīn Ṭūsī's Ethics', pp. 85–101.

25. On the interface of Shiʿism and Sufism, see S. H. Nasr, 'Shiʿism and Sufism: Their Relationship in Essence and History', in his *Sufi Essays* (London, 1970), pp. 104–120; and F. Daftary, 'Ḥasan-i Ṣabbāḥ and the Origins of the Nizārī Ismaili Movement', in *Ismailis in Medieval Muslim Societies*, pp. 181–204.

ranks of the *daʿwat* and other Ismailis with a minimum of technical vocabulary. The *Āghāz* is a more substantial text which, in its concise and measured exposition of the Qur'ānic teachings on eschatology, was probably also intended for a wider audience in the Muslim community. In a certain sense, the three texts may be regarded as introductory to the *Rawḍa* in which all their themes are woven together and elaborated in a more philosophical and comprehensive manner.

As already noted, one of Ṭūsī's primary services to the Ismailis was to render his scholarly skills to the exposition of their doctrines, especially in the context of the *qiyāma* proclaimed by Imam Ḥasan ʿAlā Dhikrihi al-Salām. As this doctrine informs and permeates all of Ṭūsī's Ismaili works, including the ones collected in this volume, it will be worthwhile at this point to briefly examine the notion of *qiyāma* in Islam generally and its interpretation by the Ismailis in particular.

The doctrine of *qiyāma*

The belief in life after death is as old as the history of human thought and it was, in all probability, one of the original impulses that gave rise to religious beliefs. In each religious tradition, be it revealed or otherwise, the conviction that human beings continue to survive in some form or another after death has resulted in a body of speculative thought generally referred to as eschatology. Consequently, all communities and schools within each religion, depending on the number and calibre of their scholars, have developed their own distinctive doctrines of eschatology.[26]

The theological and philosophical discourse on eschatology, with the exception of belief in sheer physical resurrection, depends ultimately on the belief in the soul or spirit and its survival after physical death. Without such a belief, the idea of *eschata*[27] or life in the hereafter—be it Hades, Tartarus, Gehanna, Sheol, Paradise or Hell—would be meaningless. The early pre-Socratic Greek philosophers regarded

---

26. For an overview see R. J. Zwi Werblowsky 'Eschatology', in *The Encyclopaedia of Religion*, ed. Lindsay Jones (Detroit, 2005), vol. 4, pp. 2833–2840; and J. A. MacCulloch, 'Eschatology', in *Encyclopaedia of Religion and Ethics*, ed. James Hastings (Edinburgh, 1994), pp. 373–391.

27. From the Greek *eschatos* and *eschata*, meaning the 'last' or 'last thing'.

the soul (*psyche*) as the distinguishing mark of all living things, but they held conflicting views about its nature, likening it to fire, heat, air, breath of life, and so on. It is in the works of Plato and Aristotle that we find a comprehensive exposition of the subject. Whereas Plato believed the soul to be a divine and immortal part of human beings, with intellectual, emotional and moral capacities, that survives the body, Aristotle held the soul to be intimately bound with the body as its form and actuality, and therefore perishable with the body without any prospect of an afterlife.[28] Notwithstanding Aristotle's immense influence on the development of theological and philosophical traditions in Christianity and Islam, it was the Platonic version of the soul that prevailed.

Among Muslim philosophers, the most elaborate proofs for the existence and immortality of human soul were furnished by Ibn Sīnā. Contrary to the Aristotelian thesis that soul is a form inseparable from the body, Ibn Sīnā argued that it is a sustainer (*mudabbir*) that can exist without body.[29] Apart from the philosophers, a considerable amount of Islamic literature on eschatology exists from the main Sunni and Shiʿi traditions. In Shiʿi Islam, the most substantive texts belong to the Twelver community.[30] Ismaili texts on the subject are rare, mainly because of the destruction of much of their literature by their opponents; and where they have survived, as in the case of *Āghāz wa anjām* in this volume, they are highly concise and abridged. Irrespective of their doctrinal differences and distinctive approaches to the subject, virtually all the Islamic texts are shaped profoundly by the Qurʾānic narratives on afterlife.[31] As M. R. Waldman observes, the

28. On Plato's theory of the soul, see in particular *Phaedo*, tr. R. Hackforth (Cambridge, 1955), and *The Republic*, tr. F. M. Cornford (Oxford, 1941); and for Aristotle, *De Anima*, tr. W. S. Hett (Cambridge, MA, 1936).

29. Ibn Sīnā, *al-Ishārāt wa al-tanbīhāt*, ed. S. Dunyā (Cairo, 1960), vol. 2, pp. 319–322.

30. M. A. Amir-Moezzi, 'Eschatology in Imami Shiʿism', in *Encyclopaedia Iranica*, vol. 8 (1998), pp. 575–581.

31. The main eschatological events narrated in the Qurʾān are summarized by M. R. Waldman in 'Islamic Eschatology', under 'Eschatology' in *The Encyclopedia of Religion*; and R. Arnaldez, 'Maʿād', in *The Encyclopedia of Islam*, 2nd ed. (hereafter referred to as *EI2*). See also Jane Idleman Smith and Yvonne Yazbeck Haddad, *The Islamic Understanding of Death and Resurrection* (New York, 1981).

highly imaginative evocations of the Qurʾān about the apocalyptic day when the earth will be rent apart and mankind resurrected for admission to the gardens of Paradise or consigned to the torments of Hellfire, have all the objective of persuading mankind to choose either the path of the good or its opposite:

> This marvellously wrought dichotomy underscores the need for humans to choose. Fire and Garden appear not for their own sake, but as signs of God's mercy or wrath ... One earns one's fate by choosing to adhere or not adhere to clearly specified spiritual and behavioural norms. Judgment is as fair as a business transaction: one's deeds are weighed in the balance, neither wealth nor kin availing. If one has been faithful and grateful, accepted his signs and messengers as true, prayed and given charity, one is awarded. If one has been faithless and ungrateful, given the lie to the signs and messengers, given God partners, prayed insincerely or not at all, and been selfish with and prideful of one's material goods, one is punished. In this instance of the radical transvaluation common to the monotheistic religions, what one valued is taken away and what one did not value becomes an eternal reward.[32]

The Qurʾānic term for the Resurrection, *qiyāma*, is derived from the verbal noun of the Arabic root *q-w-m*, which literally means 'to stand upright' or 'to rise'. It appears in the Qurʾān almost seventy times, denoting a range of meanings, but always in conjunction with the adverbial expression of time and thus referring to the Day of Resurrection (*yawm al-nushūr*, 25:40) at the end of time. It is used more or less synonymously with other expressions, such as the Hour (*al-sāʿa*, 7:178), the Great Day (*yawm al-ʿaẓīm*, 6:15), the Day of Rising (*yawm al-qiyāma*, 22:9) and the Day of In-gathering (*yawm al-ḥashr*, 6:128). From the same root *q-w-m*, the term *qāʾim* referring to a person appears three times in the Qurʾān (3:39; 11:100; 13:33), and *qāʾimatun* is mentioned once in conjunction with a community (3:113). It should also be noted that in Islamic literature, the subject of resurrection is generally discussed under the heading of 'the Return' (*al-maʿād*), although this term, which occurs only once in the Qurʾān (28:85), does not convey the complex semantic connotations of *qiyāma*.[33]

---

32. Waldman, ' Islamic Eschatology', pp. 2836–40.

33. See L. Gardet, 'Ḳiyāma', and R. Arnaldez, 'Maʿād', in *EI2*.

Apart from the terminological diversity deployed for *qiyāma* in the Qur'ān, there are many Prophetic traditions dealing with eschatological matters, which have been interpreted variably by Muslim commentators according to their ideological or sectarian orientations. In brief, the Sunni version commences with the first sounding of the Trumpet (*nafkh-i ṣūr*) which causes the total annihilation (*fanā'-i muṭlaq*) of the world. The second sounding revives the entire creation and the dead are physically resurrected. Then there is the in-gathering (*ḥashr*) at which point the *qiyāma* is established. Finally, there comes the Day of Judgment when the reckoning or accounting (*ḥisāb*) takes place and the fate of individuals is determined. In all cases, adherence to the religious law and virtuous conduct constitute the main criteria for salvation in the hereafter (*ākhirat*).

There is a similar succession of eschatological events in the Twelver Shi'i version of the *qiyāma*, but with the additional view (also held by a great many Sunnis), that the Day of Return (*yawm al-ma'ād*) will be preceded on earth by the advent of a messianic figure called the *mahdī* (the rightly guided one). This belief is based on certain Prophetic traditions such as: 'If there were to remain in the life of the world but one day, God would prolong that day until He sends in it a man from my community and my household (*ahl al-bayt*). His name will be the same as my name. He will fill the earth with equality and justice as it was filled with oppression and tyranny.'[34] For the Twelver Shi'is, the *mahdī* will be none other than their twelfth Imam, Muḥammad b. al-Ḥasan, who is said to have gone into occultation around 260/874.[35]

In common with other Muslim communities, the Ismailis too have a long tradition of speculative thought on the *qiyāma* since they first emerged as a distinctive Shi'i community in the 3rd/9th century. Almost all the leading authors of the pre-Fatimid and Fatimid periods, such as the Ikhwān al-Ṣafā', Abū Ya'qūb

34. A Prophetic tradition found in Sunni, Twelver Shi'i and Ismaili compilations, such as Ibn Māja, *Sunan*, *Kitāb al-jihād*, no. 11, in *Jam' jawāmi' al-aḥādith wa al-asānīd* (Liechtenstein, 2000), p. 406; Ja'far Sobhani, *Doctrines of Shi'i Islam*, tr. Reza Shah-Kazemi (London, 2001), p. 115; and al-Mu'ayyad fī al-Dīn al-Shīrāzī, *al-Majālis al-Mu'ayyadiyya*, vol. 2, ed. Ḥ. Ḥamīd al-Dīn (Oxford, 1986), no. 103, p. 17.

35. See W. Madelung, 'Al-Mahdī', *EI2*.

al-Sijistānī, al-Qāḍī al-Nuʿmān, Ḥamīd al-Dīn al-Kirmānī, al-Mu'ayyad fī al-Dīn Shīrāzī and Nāṣir-i Khusraw have contributed to Ismaili eschatological doctrines.[36] In contrast to both the Sunni and Twelver Shiʿi sources, however, there is a pronounced tendency in Ismaili writings to interpret the *qiyāma* in a spiritual and hermeneutical manner. This is evident, for example, in their assertion that it is the soul, not the body, which survives physical death and experiences the rewards and retributions of the afterlife. More significantly, in accordance with the Ismaili theory of cyclical sacred history comprising seven eras of prophetic revelations, the *qiyāma* will be initiated by the advent of the Resurrector (*qā'im*) who will end the era of exoteric (*ẓāhir*) religion and disclose to humanity its innermost, esoteric (*bāṭin*) truths.[37] Since Muḥammad was the last and final prophet-messenger of God, it is the function of the initiator of the seventh cycle to convey this message to mankind, on account of which he is designated as the 'Lord of the Resurrection' (*qā'im al-qiyāma*).[38]

The Ismaili doctrine of *qiyāma* reached its apotheosis in the early Nizārī period with the proclamation of Resurrection by Imam Ḥasan 'Alā Dhikrihi al-Salām at Alamūt on the 17th of Ramaḍān 559/8 August 1164. This is one of the most obscure events in Ismaili history, about which there are no reliable records since the bulk of Ismaili literature perished during the Mongol invasion.[39] The only reports we have come from secondary, anti-Ismaili sources of the Persian

---

36. For more details see my article, 'Notions of Paradise in the Works of Nasir al-Din Tusi' (forthcoming).

37. Ṭūsī discusses the cyclical theory in *Rawḍa*, pp. 69–70, §174–176, pp. 109–111, §320–323 and pp. 136–141§402–422. Henry Corbin produced a lengthy study of the subject in his *Cyclical Time and Ismaili Gnosis* (London, 1983), pp. 30–58.

38. W. Madelung, 'Ḳā'im Āl-i Muḥammad', *EI2*.

39. The only authentic Ismaili account of the event that has survived is in the works of Ḥasan-i Maḥmūd-i Kātib namely *Haft bāb-i Bābā Sayyidnā*, wrongly attributed to Ḥasan-i Ṣabbāḥ because of the resemblance of their forenames, and his collection of poetry known as the *Qā'imiyyāt*. The *Haft bāb* was published by W. Ivanow in his *Two Early Ismaili Treatises* (Bombay, 1933), pp. 4–44, and translated into English by Hodgson in *The Order of Assassins*, pp. 279–324. I am in the process of finalizing for publication an edition of *Dīwān-i Qā'imiyyāt*.

historians such as Juwaynī and Rashīd al-Dīn Faḍl Allāh, written more than a century after the event, and subsequently reiterated by other critics. For them, the proclamation of *qiyāma* amounted to a revocation of the Islamic *sharīʿat* (religious law) and a license for all kinds of illicit and immoral conduct which, however, are not substantiated in Ismaili sources.

As a result of such accusations from the Sunni establishment motivated by sectarian and political considerations, as well as internal developments within the Ismaili community, it became necessary for the Nizārī *daʿwat* to expound the doctrine of *qiyāma* in a manner both intellectually sound and politically defensible. The need for such a formulation became even more imperative at a time when Imam ʿAlāʾ al-Dīn was seeking a rapprochement with the Abbasid caliphate to forge a common alliance against the Mongols. The task of articulating the doctrine is likely to have fallen upon a number of scholars. The most talented and distinguished among them whose works have come down to us was Naṣīr al-Dīn Ṭūsī. His most elaborate treatment of the subject, the *Rawḍa-yi taslīm* is, in its formal structure, an encyclopaedic compendium of Ismaili philosophical theology covering a wide range of themes from cosmology, prophecy and the imamate to ethics, spirituality and psychology. But from another perspective, the entirety of *Rawḍa* can be perceived as an intellectually sophisticated and sustained meditation on the relationship between this world and the next, and the spiritual significance of *qiyāma*, as reflected in the title he chose for the book 'Paradise of Submission'.

As one would expect of someone steeped in Ismaili hermeneutics and the intellectual legacy of Imam Ḥasan ʿAlā Dhikrihi-hi Salām, Ṭūsī interprets the *qiyāma* not in a literal sense as a series of catastrophic events at the end of time, but rather as a call to the faithful to secure their spiritual resurrection and salvation here and now in the present world. The attainment of this goal, which Ṭūsī asserts is a fundamental duty of every faithful Ismaili, requires a radical transformation of one's life resulting in continuous communion with the Divine. Far from renouncing the prescriptions of the *sharīʿat*, as alleged by opponents of the Ismailis, he insists on their rigorous observance, but these rites would be rendered invalid without an understanding of their inner, spiritual significance. Anyone worshipping in a purely outward, uncomprehending way is in reality a dead person who has already been judged and condemned to Hellfire in the next world. Conversely, the one who wholly submerges his self in God and attains the state of unity (*waḥdat*) is already resurrected into new life beyond all distinctions and polarities, including those of good and evil, existence and non-existence, Heaven and Hell. Another aspect of Ṭūsī's multi-layered hermeneutical analysis in the *Rawḍa* is his theoretical construct of a series of 'relative' paradises and hells encountered by every living being in its journey towards perfection (*kamāl*).[40] In many respects, therefore, Ṭūsī's elucidation of the *qiyāma* signifies a return to the original esoteric and spiritual vision held by Ismaili authors.

The same understanding of *qiyāma* as a summons to spiritual rebirth in this world permeates all other works composed by Ṭūsī in this period of his life, including the three shorter treatises collected in this volume.

Tawallā wa tabarrā

The *Tawallā* is one of Ṭūsī's earliest Ismaili texts composed in Quhistān before his move to Alamūt. This is evident from Ṭūsī's dedication of this work to his first patron, Nāṣir al-Dīn Muḥtashim 'Abd al-Raḥīm b. Abī Manṣūr, for whom he also compiled two works on ethical philosophy, *Akhlāq-i Nāṣirī* and *Akhlāq-i Muḥtashimī*. The text of the *Tawallā* is based on Dānish-Pazhuh's excellent edition printed with *Akhlāq-i Muḥtashimī* (pp. 561–570).[41] I have made only minor corrections as recorded in the manuscript variants at the end of the Persian text.

The integral notion of *tawallā* (solidarity) and *tabarrā* (dissociation), in the manner that Ṭūsī describes here, corresponds to the Shi'i principle of *walāya*, the first pillar of the Ismaili faith as articulated by the Fatimid chief *dā'ī* al-Qāḍī al-Nu'mān in the opening chapter of his *Da'ā'im al-Islām*.[42] Essentially, *walāya* requires recognition of

40. Ṭūsī, *Rawḍa*, pp. 60–62§143–150.

41. The manuscript used by Dānish-Pazhūh is preserved in the Majlis Library, Tehran (Ms 630/12, pp. 157–158).

42. al-Qāḍī al-Nu'mān, *Da'ā'im al-Islam*, ed. A. A. A. Fyzee (Cairo, 1951–1961), 2 vols.; English trans. A. A. A. Fyzee and revised by Ismail K. Poonawala as *The*

the Imams descended from 'Alī b. Abī Ṭālib, and the demonstration of absolute devotion and obedience to them. Quoting the maxim attributed to Prophet Muḥammad, 'Religion is love and hatred for the sake of God', Ṭūsī takes solidarity with the Imams and dissociation from anything alien to them as an indispensable condition for the seekers of truth. Since faith cannot be complete or perfected without guidance of the Imam of the time, it is incumbent upon the faithful to be devoted to him who is designated by Ṭūsī as *farmāndih-i ḥaqīqat* (the truthful teacher) and *mu'allim-i dīn* (the master of religion).

Ṭūsī's object in this treatise is not merely to reaffirm an established theological principle, but to delineate the internal process by which solidarity may be cultivated and attained by the individual. At the formal, exoteric level, this involves the subordination of one's baser instincts identified with the animal soul (*nafs-i bahīmī*), such as lust and anger, to the control of the intellect (*nafs-i gūyā-yi insānī*), which in turn must be obedient to the teachings of the Imam. At the esoteric level, the process of attaining solidarity and dissociation is accompanied by a progressive psychological and spiritual transformation of one's personality, so that lust and anger turn to chastity and forbearance, and greed for wealth and social position are replaced by altruism and seclusion, until one attains the states of *riḍā* (contentment) and *taslīm* (submission). At this point, all contraries of good and bad, joy and sorrow, solidarity and disassociation disappear, and there is complete peace and composure. The final degree is that of certitude (*īqān*), when one renounces all desires of this world and the next, including the search for self-perfection, love, gnosis, even the reward and bliss of Heaven, as equal to idol-worship, for such a person recognizes nothing but the reality of God. The ultimate goal of every Ismaili, says Ṭūsī, is to perfect his faith by becoming one of the elite people of unity (*ahl-i waḥdat*). It is by way of analysing the subtle ethical and spiritual transformation engendered by solidarity and dissociation that Ṭūsī manages to convey to his readers the central message of the Ismaili

---

Pillars of Islam (New Delhi, 2002, 2004), 2 vols. See also M. A. Amir-Moezzi, '*Walāya*', in *Journal of the American Oriental Society*, 122 (2002), pp. 722–741; and Maria M. Dakake, *The Charismatic Community: Shi'ite Identity in Early Islam* (New York, 2007).

doctrine of *qiyāma*, that in order to be truly resurrected in spirit, it is necessary for the faithful to be totally and continually absorbed in contemplation of the Divine.

Maṭlūb al-muʾminīn

The second of our treatises is found in numerous manuscripts preserved among the Ismaili communities of Iran, northern Pakistan and the Badakhshan region of Tajikistan. It was first published by the late W. Ivanow in *Two Ismaili Treatises* (pp. 43–55). The present edition is based on a number of manuscripts, the oldest being the one found in Sedeh, a village near Bīrjand in southern Khurāsān. The name of the scribe and date of transcription of this manuscript are not known. Another relatively correct manuscript of the text dated 15 Ṣafar al-Muẓaffar 1352/9 June 1933 was also used in the process of editing. Apart from those of the oldest manuscript, variant readings are taken from six other manuscripts, all dated in the 19th and 20th centuries, and referred to here as 'نخ' indicating any one of these manuscripts.[43]

The *Maṭlūb al-muʾminīn* is dedicated to the august presence (*ḥaḍrat-i ʿulyā*) of the Imam ʿAlāʾ al-Dīn Muḥammad,[44] who requested the author to compile a summary of what he had read from the *Fuṣūl-i mubārak* of Imam Ḥasan ʿAlā Dhikrihi al-Salām and other *daʿwat* literature. This indicates that Ṭūsī's early works were partially inspired by the *Fuṣūl*, and that *Maṭlūb* itself was compiled either in Alamūt or the neighbouring fortress of Maymūn Dizh, sometime after the year 640/1243.

Like the *Tawallā*, the *Maṭlūb* is addressed to initiates of the Nizārī *daʿwat* and ordinary members of the community. It covers more or less the same ground, reminding them of the essentials of their faith, such as recognition of the Imam, the conditions of faithfulness, solidarity

---

43. A photocopy of the oldest manuscript along with many other manuscripts of the text is preserved in the library of The Institute of Ismaili Studies in London.

44. In his introduction to *Haft bāb* in *Two Early Ismaili Treatises,* Ivanow incorrectly translates '*ḥaḍrat-i ʿulyā*' to mean 'a noble lady from the house of Imam'. The poet Ḥasan-i Maḥmūd uses the same expression for Imam ʿAlāʾ al-Dīn in his *Dīwān-i Qāʾimiyyāt*.

and dissociation, the degrees of certitude, etc. But in contrast to the brevity of *Tawallā*, it is a longer text with four chapters, and Ṭūsī's perspective is focused much more on the idea of origin and destination (*mabdaʾ wa maʿād*) or, in his words: 'Where has man come from, why has he come, and where is he heading to?' Also, the *Maṭlūb* goes much farther in its final chapter with a discussion of the seven pillars of the Ismaili faith. In common with his Fatimid predecessors, Ṭūsī provides both the exoteric and esoteric meanings of religious rituals such as prayer, fasting, pilgrimage and *jihād*. He is careful in declaring that the observance of *sharīʿat* is obligatory for all Ismailis, but it must be performed in both their exoteric and esoteric aspects. By thus reasserting the Fatimid principle of complementarity between *ẓāhir* and *bāṭin*, Ṭūsī was undoubtedly presenting the official Ismaili understanding of the *sharīʿat* in the age of *qiyāma*. As in the *Tawallā*, Ṭūsī emphasizes the core spiritual teaching of *qiyāma* that the ultimate goal of the Ismaili is to regard all things of this world and the hereafter as illusions, and to seek only the reality of oneness with God.

Āghāz wa anjām

In some manuscripts, this treatise bears the title *Tadhkira* (Admonition), a term that also appears in Ṭūsī's introduction to the text. Numerous manuscripts of the *Āghāz* have survived and it has been published many times in the original Persian language.[45] The present edition is based on the earliest known manuscript of the text in the handwriting of Abū al-Majd Muḥammad b. Masʿūd Tabrīzī, copied almost sixty years after Ṭūsī's death, on Sunday, 11 Rabīʿ I, 723/20 March 1323, and referred to here with the letter 'S = س' indicating *Safīna-yi Tabrīz*. A lithographed edition of the *Safīna* was published in Tehran, 2003, in which *Āghāz* constitutes pp. 352–357. Apart from comparing the text with the edited version 'T = ت' of Īraj Afshār (Tehran, 1335 Sh./1956), I have also collated the text with the undated manuscript 'B = ب' of the Bodleian Library, Oxford, and 'M = م' housed in the library of the Faculty of Letters at Mashhad University, copied in Jumādā I, 1083/August 1672. The printed version of Īraj

45. An inventory of *Āghāz wa anjām* appears in the listing of the Centre for the Publication of Written Heritage, *Nashr-i mīrāth-i maktūb* (Tehran, 2008).

Afshār and other manuscripts occasionally differ from 'S', and all such variations have been recorded at the end of the Persian text.

In 1997, the Iranian scholar Ḥasan Ḥasanzādeh Āmulī published an edition along with his comments on the *Āghāz*, in which he explains the complexities of the text and its influence on the Persian schools of Ibn al-'Arabī and Ṣadr al-Dīn Shīrāzī, better known as Mullā Ṣadrā of Isfahan, and other distinguished Shi'i writers. In fact, Mullā Ṣadrā incorporated an Arabic translation of almost the entire *Āghāz* in his commentary on the Qur'ān, *Mafātīḥ al-ghayb*, without explicitly acknowledging his source.[46] While Āmulī's commentary deserves our appreciation, it fails to recognize the Ismaili terminology and exegetical aspect of the text without which the *Āghāz* cannot be fully comprehended. Moreover, Āmulī uses a version close to the edition of Īraj Afshār, which in certain areas is either defective or incomplete, hindering a sound analysis of the text.

Unlike both the *Tawallā* and *Maṭlūb* which outline the principles and practice of the Ismaili faith, the *Āghāz wa anjām* is a much more extensive and substantive text of twenty chapters wherein Ṭūsī's attention is focused almost exclusively on the Qur'ānic narratives on the hereafter, supported by copious citations of its verses, traditions of the Prophet and the Imams, and other sources of both Arabic and Persian provenance. In this respect, the *Āghāz* can be further distinguished from the *Rawḍa* where, notwithstanding the author's profound engagement with the notion of *qiyāma*, such citations are comparatively few and far between, presumably because it was addressed to an educated elite of the *da'wat* already familiar with the proof-texts of the Qur'ān and other sources of authority on the subject.

In his preamble to the *Āghāz*, Ṭūsī admits to the difficulty of writing about the hereafter, since his intention is to record an account 'not as rendered by scholars but by men of insight (*ahl-i bīnish*)'. In the first four chapters, he establishes the intellectual groundwork by exploring the basic issues of human origin and destination, existence and non-existence, perfection and deficiency, the relationship between the corporeal and spiritual worlds, the hidden and the manifest, the

46. See Ḥasan H. Āmulī, *Āghāz wa anjām-i Khawāja Naṣīr al-Dīn Ṭūsī: Muqaddima wa sharḥ wa ta'līqāt* (Qumm, 1366 Sh./1997), especially pp. 78–80 where he identifies almost all the instances where Mullā Ṣadrā quotes and elaborates upon Ṭūsī's text.

nature of time and space, etc. The spiritual realm is much more real than, and superior to, all aspects of the physical realm. It is the realm of truth, reality and certainty, exalted above time and place. In order to obtain salvation, one needs to absolutely discard the physical world and be resurrected in the spirit. This is a process Ṭūsī calls 'the secret of the Resurrection (*sirr-i qiyāmat*)' which is hidden even to the prophets, and cannot be explained by mere 'partial intelligence' or the 'exoterics of the revelation', but rather with a kind of intelligence which Ṭūsī, following Imam Ḥasan 'Alā Dhikrihi al-Salām, calls the 'Resurrectional intelligence of the Hereafter (*'aql-i qiyāmati-yi ākhiratī*)'.[47]

In the chapters that follow, Ṭūsī embarks on a systematic and highly condensed exegesis of the Qur'ānic verses on eschatology, ranging across a broad spectrum of themes from the soundings of the Trumpet and the in-gathering for Resurrection, to the reading of the Scroll of Deeds, Heaven and Hell, angels and satans, the rivers of Paradise, the Tree of Bliss and its counterpart the Infernal Tree, the virgins of Paradise, etc. Throughout his discourse, Ṭūsī maintains a highly subtle, dialectical balance between the exoteric and esoteric readings of the Qur'ān, between fidelity to the letter of the text and its inner, spiritual meaning. In contrast to the elaborate philosophical analysis of the *Rawḍa*, Ṭūsī's construction of the *Āghāz* is highly compressed and terse in style, perhaps reflecting the difficulties inherent in dealing with a subject so complex and enigmatic as the afterlife, as he alludes in the Preamble:

> ... not all that exists is destined for everyone, and not everyone can see what is destined for him, nor can one know all that one sees, nor can one express [in speech] all one knows, and not everyone can write all that he can express. Because, if seeing is by direct vision (*bi'ayn*), knowing can only be a trace (*athar*); if knowledge is conceiving, speaking can only be by informing; and if speech is explicit (*bi taṣrīḥ*), writing can only be by implication and allusion.

Ṭūsī concludes the treatise with a reminder of the core message of the *qiyāma* that appears in all his Ismaili works that the people of this world who have attained absolute certainty and unity of purpose with the Divine are already resurrected and liberated in spirit. In effect,

47. Ṭūsī, *Rawḍa*, pp. 81§221 and 83§231.

they have overcome all contraries, surpassed their longing for Heaven and fear of Hell, and ventured beyond the prospects of reward and retribution. Apparently for Ṭūsī, the essence of the Resurrection is encapsulated in the famous Prophetic tradition which he quotes in the *Āghāz* (§92), *Tawallā* (§18) and *Maṭlūb* (§12):

> This world is forbidden to the people of the Hereafter, and the Hereafter is forbidden to the people of this world, and both of them are forbidden to the people of God.

From a theological perspective, therefore, the *Āghāz wa anjām* may be considered as a significant effort on the part of Ṭūsī to convey the spiritual meaning of the Ismaili doctrine of the Resurrection. While his interpretation is consistent with Qur'ānic teachings, it nevertheless draws conclusions which are distinct from those of the Sunni and the Twelver Shi'i authors.

Note on the edition and translation

In this edition, apart from applying contemporary Persian orthographical conventions, I have corrected spelling errors, eliminated faulty readings and, in a number of instances, reconstructed the text as indicated within square brackets [ ] in the original Persian. Manuscript variants containing a sentence or a phrase are enclosed within angles <>, and the absence of this sign signifies variation in one word of the text. To facilitate cross-reference between the Persian and English texts, passages that deal with a single or group of related ideas have been numbered and identified in both versions of the text with the section sign [§].

The English translation aims to be a close rendering of the original Persian. In the case of *Āghāz*, which is a bi-lingual text, numerous Qur'ānic verses are embedded in the body of the text so that in many cases they appear as part of Ṭūsī's sentence structure. To distinguish Qur'ānic verses from the main text they appear boldface in the Persian text and italics in the English translation, together with their chapter and verse numbers. I have consulted various translations of the Qur'ān for the purpose of this publication, but the verse numbers conform to that of Yusuf Ali's system.

On many occasions, Ṭūsī cites in Arabic traditions of the Prophet and Imams, as well other sources which he does not identify. In the translation, I have displayed these reports within quotes and, wherever possible, endeavoured to locate the provenance of these reports. In a number of cases, I have simply reported 'Text in Arabic', meaning that it is an aphorism of anonymous origin, but which Ṭūsī considered sufficiently authoritative to incorporate in his writing with minor rephrasing. Occasionally, Ṭūsī provides a Persian translation of an Arabic text which is usually a very close version of the original. In order to avoid repetition I have, in many cases, not conveyed Ṭūsī's Persian translations. Also, the terms which have found their way into the English lexicon have not been transliterated. Occasionally, to render a more coherent translation, I have added a word or phrase to the translation within square brackets.

The system of transliteration adopted for the Persian and Arabic scripts is a modified version of the one used in the 2nd edition of the *Encyclopaedia of Islam*, except for the letter dj, Ḳ and č, which have been replaced by j, q and ch, and the ligatures have been dispensed with. Dates are given according to both the Islamic and Common calendars; in the notes and bibliography some publication dates are given according to the solar Islamic calendar of Iran and marked 'Sh' for Shamsī.

Tawallā wa tabarrā
Solidarity and Dissociation

In the Name of God the Beneficent, the Merciful

God be praised who is the Cherisher and Sustainer of the worlds.
Peace be upon our lord Muḥammad and his blessed progeny.

[§1] For anyone seeking steadfastness in religion, two things are indispensable: one is solidarity (*tawallā*) and the other is dissociation (*tabarrā*). As [the Prophet] has said: 'Religion is love and hate for the sake of God.'[48] To begin with, our brother in faith, Najīb al-Dīn Ḥasan[49]—may God grant him success and fulfil his wishes—beseeched this humble person Muḥammad-i Ṭūsī to write an essay on the subject and there was no alternative but to compose a few words for him from the sayings of the leaders of religion (*pīshwāyān-i dīn*) and instructors of the people of certainty (*muʿallimān-i ahl-i yaqīn*), especially the present instructor (*muʿallim-i waqt*), the exalted king, helper of religion and state, king of Iran ʿAbd al-Raḥīm b. Abī Manṣūr[50]—may God exalt his sovereignty and protect his blessed existence.

[§2] We begin by saying that mankind possesses two faculties which are subsidiaries and branches of the animal soul (*nafs-i bahīmī*), namely lust and anger (*shahwat wa ghaḍab*), that is [in Persian], *ārazū* and *khashm*. These two faculties also exist in other animals, and 'to do' and 'not to do' are the outcome of these two faculties. But mankind possesses another soul which does not exist in other animals, namely the rational soul (*nafs-i nāṭiqa*), and also [a kind] of intelligence which in Persian is translated as *khirad* (wisdom).

[§3] It is essential that the animal soul, whose faculties are lust and anger, should be subservient to the human rational soul (*nafs-i gūyāy-i insānī*). The rational soul should be subservient to the intellect,

48. A Prophetic tradition cited in M. M. Narāqī, ed. M. Riḍā Āl-i Muẓaffar, *Jāmiʿ al-saʿādāt* (Najaf, 1963), vol. 3, pp. 183–184.

49. I have been unable to find more information about this person other than that he was evidently a senior Ismaili *dāʿī* in Quhistān where Ṭūsī composed this treatise.

50. This was Ṭūsī's patron in Quhistān, Nāṣir al-Dīn ʿAbd al-Raḥīm b. Abī Manṣūr (d. 655/1257).

and the intellect should abide by the commandment of the truthful commander (*farmāndih-i ḥaqīqat*)[51] who is called the teacher of religion (*muʿallim-i dīn*), so that action is aligned with rectitude (*istiqāmat*). If this were contradicted, action would be diverted and without rectitude. In other words, the intellect would be subservient to the rational soul, [and] the rational soul would be subservient to the animal soul, [which] leads to the pursuit of lust and anger, and consequently collapses into blazing fire (*hāwiya*) which is called Hell. We seek refuge in God from this.

[§4] Thus, when the animal soul abides by the commandment of the rational soul, lust and anger become more subtle; lust evolves and reaches the state of yearning (*shawq*), and anger evolves and reaches the state of aversion (*iʿrāḍ*). Consequently, the one whose rational soul subdues his animal soul would, instead of lust and anger, possess yearning and aversion. When the rational soul falls subservient to the commandment of intellect, yearning and aversion become more refined and perfect and are transformed into liking (*irādat*) and disliking (*karāhat*). [And] when intellect falls subservient to the commandment of the truthful commander (*farmāndih-i ḥaqīqat*), liking and disliking are transformed into solidarity and dissociation (*tawallā wa tabarrā*).

[§5] The epitome of solidarity is directing oneself towards someone (*rūy farā kasī kardan ast*), and the epitome of dissociation is abandoning all that is apart from him. One reaches this state when one's lust and anger turn into love directed towards someone, and animosity and dislike towards all that is apart from him. Otherwise, when the rational soul falls subservient to the animal soul, two other things will be added to lust and anger, namely love for wealth and love for position. And when intellect falls subservient to the rational soul, two other things will be added to it, namely greed and arrogance. [All] other base ethics will result from this and man will be taken to such a position where there is no bad quality in existence that is not

51. A synonym for the Ismaili Imam, as are also the terms *muʿallim-i dīn* (teacher of religion), *āmir-i amr* (commander of the command), *mard-i khudā* (man of God) and *muḥiqq-i yagāna* (unique truthful person) used elsewhere in the text.

present in him. That will end up in eternal ruin. We seek refuge in God from this.

[§6] But in the person whose action is straight, when the animal soul drives him towards lust, the rational soul which is dominant turns that lust into chastity (*ʿiffat*), the meaning of which is purity of soul. And when his animal soul drives him towards anger, the rational soul turns that anger into forbearance (*ḥilm*), the meaning of which is patience and restraint. When the rational soul drives the person towards love for wealth, the intellect turns that into altruism (*īthār*), the meaning of which is giving preference to others over oneself. When the rational soul drives one towards love for position, the intellect turns that into seclusion (*ʿuzlat*) and isolation (*inqiṭāʿ*), that is, avoiding masses. And when the [intellect] drives one towards greed, the commander of the command (*āmir-i amr*) will turn that greed into contentment (*qanāʿat*), and when driving towards arrogance, the commander will turn that into humility (*tawāḍuʿ*). These commendable qualities will act as foundations for other ethics, leading to a situation where all good qualities that are possible in mankind will be attained and the one who possesses them will reach the eternal bliss (*saʿādat-i abadī*). May our lord desire that!

[§7] Solidarity and dissociation have their respective exoteric and esoteric aspects. The exoteric aspect of solidarity is to face good people and that of dissociation is to detest bad people. The esoteric aspect of solidarity is to face the man of God (*mard-i khudā*), that is, that unique truthful person (*muḥiqq-i yagāna*) who is the foundation of all good things, and that of dissociation is to detest all that which is apart from him.

[§8] Two things make solidarity possible, gnosis and affection (*maʿrifat wa maḥabbat*), because those who fail to recognize God and to love Him may not come before Him. Recognition is gnosis and affection is love. Dissociation is also made possible by two things: emigration (*hijrat*) and endeavour (*jihād*). Emigration is cutting off from everything apart from God and endeavour is making an effort, because unless one cuts off from everything apart from God and strives against His enemies, dissociation will not be complete.

[§9] [Of] the above four things, namely gnosis, love, emigration and endeavour, without which solidarity and dissociation are incomplete, each one has an exoteric and an esoteric aspect. The exoteric [aspect] of gnosis is to recognize God; its esoteric [aspect] is to recognize nothing except Him. The exoteric [aspect] of love is to love God; its esoteric is to love nothing except Him. The exoteric [aspect] of emigration is to cut off from His enemies; its esoteric is to cut off from everything other than Him, particularly oneself and one's personal likings. The exoteric [aspect] of endeavour is making an effort against God's enemies and to devote in His path one's wealth, position, wife and children; [its esoteric aspect] is to bring down to nothing one's lust and anger, one's love for possession and position, and one's likes and dislikes in His path.[52] Once one accomplishes the above requirements, the conditions of solidarity and dissociation are fulfilled, and what remains is the perfection of religiosity which depends on contentment (*riḍā*) and submission (*taslīm*).

[§10] Contentment and submission are realized when solidarity and dissociation become one and the same thing, that is, dissociation is submerged into solidarity. This is similar to when relativity (*iḍāfat*) is submerged into reality (*ḥaqīqat*), the achievable (*musta'naf*) into the primordial (*mafrūgh*), and religious law (*sharīʿat*) into resurrection (*qiyāmat*), until absolute solidarity (*tawallā-yi ṣirf*) is attained. Such a solidarity and dissociation would include the solidarity and dissociation that one had in the first instance, and this can only be realized when one's likes and dislikes become one and the same thing. Dislike is submerged into like, resulting in love and gnosis: to become

52. In *Rawḍa* (p. 84§235) Ṭūsī interprets endeavour in the path of God (*jihād*) as follows: '…at the time of the Prophet Muḥammad, people were summoned to Paradise on condition that they sacrificed their bodies and wealth. Subsequently they were summoned to esoteric instruction (*taʿlīm*) on condition that they sacrificed their bodies and wealth, [as well as] their anger and lust. Later on they were summoned to [obey] a person [that is, the Imam] on condition that they sacrificed their bodies, wealth, anger and lust, [as well as] their knowledge and intellect. Still later they were summoned to the Lord [of the Resurrection] on condition that they spontaneously forsake and abnegate their own selves, drowning in that [sacrifice] all their physical well-being, wealth, lust, anger, knowledge and intelligence.'

one and the same thing, that is, love is submerged into gnosis. If one sees no one except Him, from whom is one dissociating oneself? And if one recognizes no one except Him, what else should be the object of one's desire?

[§11] Once things are like this, all one's worldly affairs will be the same and one will be content with whatever happens. No happiness can make one happy and no sadness can cause grief. One will not feel regret for the past, nor have [false] hopes for the future. Such being the case, one will have obtained the status of contentment (*riḍā*), which is the same as the status of satisfaction (*khushnūdī*), meaning that whatever happens, one will be content and pleased with God and, as such, one can expect that God may be pleased with him.[53]

[§12] The signs of contentment are three. First, whatever befalls one, be it good or bad, one should not exhibit joy or ill feeling. Second, one should abide by whatever one is commanded to do it, whether pleasant or unpleasant, without exhibiting objection or dismay. Because it is the commandment of the truthful commander, one should not feel any difference, that is, prefer one side over the other. For example, if one is commanded to make someone happy or harm someone, one should not feel a difference. The third that one should not reject any creature and exhibit aversion (*nifrat*); one should not say 'This one is good, that one is bad, this one is a charitable person, that one is an evildoer'. Rather, one should act and do according to whatever one is instructed to say and whatever is revealed to one's heart to do, since it is from the teacher of religion (*muʿallim-i dīn*), [and] one should learn and should not, under any circumstance, act independently. When one finds these signs in oneself, the status of contentment (*riḍā*) has been reached.

[§13] What remains [is the fulfilment of] submission (*taslīm*). Submission means to surrender (*bāz supurdan bāshad*). The implication of surrender is such that one must dispense with things that cannot accompany one to the Hereafter; one should consider them borrowed and unreal (*majāzī*), for example, eyes, ears, tongue, hand and foot, indeed the whole body, desire, passion, anger, likes, dislikes, and

53. Alluding to the Qur'ānic verses 89: 27–28.

internal faculties such as estimation (*wahm*), knowledge and insight (*bīnish*). All these and all things associated with them, such as wealth, position, honour, dignity and so on, even one's life and livelihood (*jān wa zindagānī*), all such things should be considered as borrowed. For example, someone entrusted to take care of another person's property craves for it to be taken away from him and feels at ease when this happens. One should be happy that a great burden is removed from one's heart and relieved from a great misery when an obligation is fulfilled. Thus, when one reaches such a state when all the [worldly] things around one become worthless and one feels no attachment to them, one has reached the state of submission (*taslīm*).

[§14] Once solidarity, dissociation, contentment and submission are acquired, faith is obtained (*īmān ḥāṣil āmada bāshad*). Otherwise, one cannot be called faithful (*mu'min*). As it is revealed [in the Qur'ān]: '*But no, by their Lord, they will not believe until they make you* [the Prophet] *the judge in all disputes between them, and find no resistance against your verdict, but accept it with the fullest conviction*' (4:65).

[§15] In [the above verse], three conditions have been set for the faithful. The first is recognition of authority (*taḥkīm*), meaning accepting [the Prophet's] sovereignty over oneself, which is solidarity, the type which encompasses both solidarity and dissociation. The second and third are contentment and submission. Once one reaches this rank, he becomes a man of faith (*mu'min*). What remains is to reach [the rank of] being certain (*mūqin*). The relationship of the man of faith with this world is the same as the relationship of the man of certitude with the Hereafter, as it is revealed [in the Qur'ān]: '*Those who believe in the unseen and have assurance of the Hereafter*' (2:3–4).

[§16] Faith means believing and certitude is arriving at certainty. Occasionally, belief may be associated with doubt (*bā ẓann buwad*), but certainty is devoid of doubt. Doubt relates to worldly affairs, while certitude relates to the Hereafter, as has been explained in a number of places in the Sacred Words (*Kalām-i muqaddas*, that is, the *Fuṣūl* of Imam Ḥasan 'Alā Dhikrihi al-Salām]. Certitude is such that one knows the Hereafter as if looking at it, and this will only happen when one has witnessed the non-existence of the [physical] world and its conditions.

[§17] Thus, if one considers this world as [real] existence, one's vision will be reversed, and undoubtedly he will consider the Hereafter as non-existence. If one considers the Hereafter as [real] existence, one will see this world as non-existent, because these two necessitate one another. Thus, the man of certitude is the one who sees this world and its affairs as non-existent, and the more he severs his attachment to it, [the more] his certainty of the Hereafter will increase.

[§18] Certitude also has three stages: one is *ḥaqq-i yaqīn*, that is, the veracity of certainty; another is *ʿilm-i yaqīn*, that is, the realization of certainty; and the third is the certainty itself (*ʿayn-i yaqīn*), that is, its essence and reality. Veracity of certainty is the position of those men of faith who in this world are facing the Hereafter. Realization of certainty is the rank of those who have attained perfection of the Hereafter. The essence and reality of certainty is the rank of those who surpass the Hereafter. They are called the people of unity (*ahl-i waḥdat*). In this context [the Prophet] said: 'This world is forbidden to the people of the Hereafter, and the Hereafter is forbidden to the people of this world, and both of them are forbidden to the people of God.'[54]

[§19] Man can reach the rank of unity when he abandons both existence and non-existence, and his vision surpasses these two stations. As long as one commutes between existence and non-existence, he can either be a man of this world or a man of the Hereafter. If he desires illusory existence and real non-existence, he is a man of this world and the Hereafter is forbidden to him. If he desires true existence and illusory non-existence, he is the man of the Hereafter and this world is forbidden to him. If he desires neither existence nor non-existence, that is, he neither wants self nor selflessness, nor does he know or see any of these two, he will be a man of God, and both this world and the Hereafter are forbidden to him.

---

54. A Prophetic tradition cited in Suyūṭī, *al-Jāmiʿ al-ṣaqīr fī aḥādith al-bashīr al-nadhīr*, ed. ʿAbd al-Raʾūf al-Munāwī (Cairo, 1954), vol. 2, p. 17. See also Mīrzā Laʿl Bayk Badakhshī, *Thamarāt al-quds min shajarāt al-uns*, ed. Kamāl Ḥāj-Sayed-Jawādī (Tehran, 1997), p. 1331.

[§20] In other words, if one desires this world or the Hereafter, one will fall from the perfection of the degree [of being the man of God] and becomes ill-fated, because, as long as one yearns for the Hereafter, Paradise, reward and bliss, one is seeking one's own perfection. If one desires self-perfection, one loves oneself and not God, and he will be the man of multiplicity (*kathrat*) and not of unity (*waḥdat*), as has been said: 'Whatever you see apart from God, it is an idol; destroy it!'[55]

[§21] Thus, loving anything but God is idol worship. The Hereafter, Paradise, contentment and proximity of God (*jawār-i khudā*) are all apart from God. Therefore, the seeker of unity should neither indulge nor desire such things or even find his self among those who do so, because the sign for anyone who recognizes God is that he does not want anything except God. Moreover, even seeking gnosis and loving God is in itself multiplicity, because in [the realm of] unity, there is neither knowing nor known, neither lover nor beloved. All will be God and God alone.

[§22] Thus, the one who only sees God and nothing else will be the seeker of unity (*ṭālib-i waḥdat*). When God Almighty removes the veils of existence and non-existence from him, he will reach this degree, and this is a rank that no creature can describe. That which can be described in words cannot be free from denial (*kufr*) and ascribing partners to God (*shirk*). Thus, the seeker (*mujtahid*) should try to remove from him all that is apart from God, so that he, by his own endeavour, may reach the reality of his own self, God Almighty willing.

[§23] This is what he [Ṭūsī] compiled in his own handwriting.[56]

---

55. From a verse of Sanāʾī, *Dīwān*, ed. M. Taqī Mudarris-i Raḍawī (Tehran, 1365 Sh./1986, rep. 2006), p. 52.

56. An earlier version of this translation of the *Tawallā* appeared in Hermann Landolt, Samira Sheikh and Kutub Kassam (ed.) *An Anthology of Ismaili Literature: A Shiʿi Vision of Islam* (London, 2008), pp. 241–246.

Maṭlūb al-muʾminīn
Desideratum of the Faithful

In the Name of God the Beneficent, the Merciful

God be praised, who led us to His own gnosis, taught us how to be thankful, and out of His own compassion opened a gate from among the gates of knowledge to us, and guided us to the sincerity in the confession of His Oneness.

[§1] Although this most humble servant of the rightly guiding summons (*daʿwat-i hādiya*),[57] Muḥammad-i Ṭūsī, does not consider himself competent to talk about knowledge [of religion], but since the august position (*ḥaḍrat ʿulyā*)[58]—may its command be obeyed at all times—has indicated that for faithful seekers, a compilation of what I have read in the *Fuṣūl-i mubārak*,[59] books of adherents of the religion (*kutub-i ahl-i dīn*), and have heard from the instructors (*muʿallimān*),[60] should be composed, a selection from the *Fuṣūl-i mubārak* and books of the leaders of religion (*kutub-i pīshwāyān-i dīn*) is therefore compiled in a manner that its understanding may not be difficult for the seekers of the true path (*rāh-i ḥaqq*).

[§2] Since the composition of the human body cannot be devoid of four basic elements [earth, water, air and fire], this brief compilation is also divided into four chapters. It is named *Maṭlūb al-muʾminīn* (Desideratum of the Faithful), and my expectation

57. The term *daʿwat* (Arabic *daʿwa*) refers to the 'call', 'summons' or 'invitation' to follow the right religion, as exemplified in the Qurʾānic verse: '*Invite to the path of God with wisdom and beautiful preaching, and reason with them in the best of ways*' (16:125). Among the Ismailis, it was applied to the organization for propagating the faith, formally known as *daʿwat-i hādiya*, 'the rightly-guided mission'. Ṭūsī uses the word with varied meanings, such as preaching, mission or religion, according to the context. On the evolution and organization of the Ismaili *daʿwat* in its Fatimid and Nizārī forms, see Daftary, *The Ismāʿīlīs*, Chapters 3, 4 and 6.

58. The 'august position' refers to the Imam ʿAlāʾ al-Dīn Muḥammad in his capacity as the supreme head of the *daʿwat*. See note 44 above.

59. On *Fuṣūl-i mubārak*, see note 5 above.

60. This may refer to senior *dāʿī*s and scholars of the Nizārī *daʿwat* of the time, such as Nāṣir al-Dīn Muḥtashim, Muḥtashim Shihāb, Muẓaffar b. Muḥammad and Muẓaffar b. Muʾayyad, whose association with Ṭūsī is documented in *Sayr wa sulūk*.

from the bounteous nature of my lords, dear friends, companions and brothers—May God increase their success in good deeds—is such that when this compilation is presented to their blessed sights, if they find a weak expression, an oversight or a mistake, they should attribute it to this lowly servant, correct the mistakes and, out of their bounteous nature, look at it with the eye of forbearance. And if expressions and meanings are found to be befitting, they should consider it a blessing from the lord of the time (*khudawand-i zamān*),[61] accept and listen to it, and offer an affectionate prayer for this humble and needful [author].

Contents of the Book:

Chapter 1: On origin and destination
Chapter 2: Description of the faithful Ismaili
Chapter 3; On solidarity and dissociation
Chapter 4: On the seven pillars of religious law and their esoteric interpretation

Chapter 1
On origin and destination

[§3] Men of wisdom should recognize that the origin of mankind is God Almighty's Command (*amr-i bārī taʿālā*) through the mediation of Intellect, Soul, spheres, stars and effects of natural constitutions (*ṭabāyiʿ*). And this lower world (*ʿālam-i suflī*) is a trace or vestige (*athar*) of the higher realm (*ʿālam-i ʿulwī*). By comprehending divine wisdom and reflecting upon the outcome of intellectual investigation, it becomes evident that God's [ultimate] aim in the creation of the world is mankind. This is confirmed by the aphorism: 'Had it not been for you, I would not have created the universe.'[62] Also, the [kind of] knowledge and awareness that exists in the human being is absent in spheres, stars, minerals and

61. The term *khudāwand-i zamān* refers to the Nizārī Imam. See note 51 above.

62. A Prophetic tradition which also appears in *Nahj al-balāgha*, ed. Ṣubḥī al-Ṣāliḥ (Beirut, 1967), p. 184 and cited in Narāqī, *Jāmiʿ al-saʿādāt*, vol. 3, pp. 183–184.

the rest of the animal kingdom. Thus, God has chosen man from among the entire animal kingdom, as revealed [in the Qurʾān]: '*We have honoured the sons of Adam and have made them sovereign on land and sea*' (17:70).

[§4] Since mankind's origin is the Command of the Necessary Existent (*wājib al-wujūd*),[63] which is the most noble essence (*jawhar*), it is obligatory for man—in order to avoid annihilation of his own existence and of the created world—to know properly his own origin and destination (*mabdaʾ wa maʿād*), that is: where has he come from, why has he come, and where is he heading to?

[§5] Such a situation cannot be realized without recognition (*maʿrifat*) of the Almighty God—something that cannot be achieved except through the Prophet, peace be upon him, and his true offspring (*farzand-i bi-ḥaqīqat*), which is the Imam of the time, that is, God's vicegerent (*khalīfa-yi khudā*), [the Prophet's] legatee (*waṣī*), and the person who stands in his place (*qāʾim maqām*). This is confirmed [in the Qurʾān]: '*I will appoint a vicegerent on earth*' (2:30), and the tradition (*khabar*) of Prophet [Muḥammad], peace be upon him: 'If the earth were devoid of the Imam of the time it would be convulsed with all its inhabitants.'[64]

[§6] Once one recognizes his Creator, and obtains knowledge of the Prophet and the Imam of the time (*imām-i zamān*), his origin and destination becomes known. The obligation that remains is to fulfil the provisions of obedience and servitude (*farmānbardārī*), that is, to comply with the words of God: '*I did not create jinn and men except to worship Me*' (51:56).

[§7] Now, worship depends on gnosis (*maʿrifat*), and gnosis cannot be obtained through intellect alone, because gnosis and all other human crafts cannot be learned without instruction (*taʿlīm*). Thus, first of all,

---

63. The term 'Necessary Existent' (*wājib al-wujūd*) is a hallmark of Ibn Sīnā's philosophy, which Ṭūsī also uses for God in *Rawḍa*, p. 16§1, and *Maṭlūb*, §4.

64. A Prophetic tradition cited in Sunni and Shiʿi sources such as Ibn Ḥanbal, *al-Musnad*, ed. M. Shākir (Cairo, 1949), vol. 4, p. 96; al-Kulaynī, *al-Uṣūl min al-Kāfī*, Arabic ed. and Persian trans. Muḥammad Bāqir Kamaraʾī (Tehran, 1956, repr. 1972), vol. 1, p. 342; and al-Qāḍī al-Nuʿmān, *Daʿāʾim*, vol. 1, p. 25; trans., p. 34.

since the recognition of God, the Exalted, is the most difficult issue, the truth demands that in this matter one needs an instructor, and that the [chain of] instructors should end up with an instructor who does not need a book [for] acquiring gnosis at all.

[§8] Thus, for an entity which is God's purpose for the creation of the world, it will not be befitting (*wājib nakunad*) to neglect [God's] commands and prohibitions (*awāmir wa nawāhī*) and indulge in beastly habits of eating, sleeping and being content with carnal desires, so much so, as to fall below the status of animals, similar to what appears in the word of the Exalted: '*Nay, they are but like cattle; nay, they are worse, astray in the path*' (25:44).

[§9] Thus, whenever the wise one abides by the command of the Imam of the time, follows the directive of the truthful instructor (*muʿallim-i ṣādiq*) and spends his possessions, family attachments, and body and soul—all of which are borrowed (*ʿāriyat*) things—in the path of truth and totally abandons his own self, he will be returning from this illusory world to the eternal world of real existence (*ʿālam-i lā-yazālī-yi wujūd-i ḥaqīqī*). As mentioned in the adage: 'Everything will return to its origin.' Such a person will have reached his abode of destination. These are, as explained, conditions for the origin and the destination.

Chapter 2
Description of the faithful Ismaili

[§10] Those who seek the true religion (*dīn-i ḥaqq*) and name themselves Ismailis should be aware of the conditions for faithfulness (*muʾminī*) and being an Ismaili. To be an Ismaili means that the claimant should possess three signs. First, he should have obtained the recognition of the Imam of the time, abide by the commands of the truthful teacher, and never abandon, even for a moment, thought and remembrance of God the Exalted (*fikr wa dhikr-i ḥaqq taʿālā*). The second [sign] is contentment (*riḍā*), meaning that whatever befalls upon him, be it good or evil, benefit or loss, he should not change his attitude. The third [sign] is submission (*taslīm*), the meaning of which is to surrender. This means that all things that one cannot carry with himself to the Hereafter should be considered borrowed things (*'āriyat*), that is, something that one should get rid of. One should devote worldly possessions, family attachments and all other worldly things to the path of truth (*rāh-i ḥaqq*), so as to reach the rank of faithfulness (*mu'minī*), in compliance with [the words of the Qur'ān]: '*But no, by their Lord, they will not believe until they make you* [the Prophet] *the judge in all disputes between them, and find no resistance against your verdict, but accept it with the fullest conviction*' (4:65).

[§11] Thereafter, one must arrive at certitude (*mūqin bāyad shudan*). This requires '*believing in the unseen*' (2:3) and '*being certain of the Hereafter*' (2:4). The man of certainty (*mūqin*) also possesses three signs: the first is veracity of certainty (*ḥaqq-i yaqīn*); the second is knowledge of certainty (*'ilm-i yaqīn*); and the third is certainty itself (*'ayn-i yaqīn*). The first is the rank of those men of faith who from this world face the Hereafter; the second is the rank of those who have reached the rank of perfection of the Hereafter; the third is the rank of those who have surpassed this world and the Hereafter, and they are the people of unity (*ahl-i waḥdat*).

[§12] The rank of unity can only be achieved when men of faith completely discard their own existence, desiring neither Paradise nor reward or perfection for themselves. They should surpass this world and the Hereafter. The Prophet [Muḥammad], peace be upon him, said: 'This world is forbidden to the people of the Hereafter, and the Hereafter is forbidden to the people of this world, and both of them are forbidden to the people of God the Exalted.'[65] These are, as narrated above, the provisions for being a faithful Ismaili.

Chapter 3
On solidarity and dissociation

[§13] For anyone claiming religiosity, two things are indispensable. The first is solidarity (*tawallā*) and the second is dissociation (*tabarrā*), as narrated from [the Prophet]: 'Religion is love and hate

65. See note 54 above.

for the sake of God.'[66] The reality of solidarity is facing someone and the reality of dissociation is discarding everyone apart from him.

[§14] Both solidarity and dissociation have their respective exoteric and esoteric [aspects]. The exoteric aspect of solidarity is facing good people and its esoteric is facing the man of God (*mard-i khudā*), that is, the Imam of the time. The exoteric meaning of dissociation is discarding and abandoning bad people and its esoteric meaning is to dislike everything apart from God.

[§15] The fulfilment of solidarity and dissociation depends on four things: first, gnosis (*ma'rifat*); second, love (*maḥabbat*); third, emigration (*hijrat*); and fourth endeavour (*jihād*), each of which having its own exoteric and esoteric [aspects]. The exoteric aspect of gnosis is to recognize God through the man of God, that is, the Imam of the time who is God's vicegerent. Its esoteric aspect is to recognize no one apart from him. The exoteric aspect of love is to have affection for him, and its esoteric aspect is to love no one apart from him. The exoteric aspect of emigration is to despise and detach oneself from the enemies of the Imam, and its esoteric aspect is to cut oneself off from everything which is apart from him like wealth, family dependents (*'iyāl*), and body and soul. The exoteric aspect of endeavour is to hate the enemies of Truth (*ḥaqq*), and its esoteric aspect is to try to abandon [worldly] lusts and pleasures and sacrifice them in the path of Truth (*rāh-i ḥaqq*). Once these objectives are fulfilled, the true solidarity and dissociation will be realized, and these are the conditions for solidarity and dissociation.

Chapter 4
On the seven pillars of religious law and their esoteric interpretation

[§16] It is evident to all groups that everything in existence has an esoteric and an exoteric aspect, and one cannot reach the esoteric aspect of anything before fulfilling its exoteric aspect. For example, the lower world (*'ālam-i suflī*) is the realm of the exoteric, and its

66. See note 48 above.

esoteric is the higher realm (*'ālam-i 'ulwī*); and anything that exists in this lower world, which is the exoteric realm, will attain [its real] existence in the esoteric realm.[67]

[§17] As for the exoteric aspect of the religious law (*ẓāhir-i sharī'at*), first the crust (*pūst*) is formed, then the pulp, seed and fruit, the aim which is perfection. Therefore, anyone claiming God's worship, must first externally abide by the rules of the religious law (*sharī'at*), which is like the crust, then follow the commandments and prohibitions of the seven pillars of religious law (*haft arkān-i sharī'at*), as prescribed by the religious law. Having performed the external aspects of the fundamentals (*arkān-i ẓāhirī*) and wishing to know its esoteric meaning, and with knowledge return from this world to the realm of the esoteric and reach one's original abode (*maqām-i aṣlī*), one should perform the seven pillars of the truth (*haft arkān-i ḥaqīqat*) in order to be considered as a man of truth (*mard-i ḥaqīqat*).

[§18] The first is attestation to faith (*shahādat*), which implies knowing God through the Imam of the time, in compliance with: '*I will appoint a vicegerent on earth*' (2:30). The second is ritual cleanliness (*ṭahārat*), which means dissociating oneself from previous religious customs and traditions, considering the command of the Imam of the time as truth (*ḥaqq*) and abiding by his command, in compliance with the words of God, the Exalted: '*Obey God and obey the Apostle and those charged with authority among you*' (4:59). The third is ritual prayer (*namāz*), meaning that even for a single breath, one should not be negligent of obedience to God and God's vicegerent so that one might be perpetually in the state of prayer, in compliance with: '*Those who remain steadfast to their prayer*' (70:23). The fourth is ritual fasting (*rūza*), meaning that one has to surrender his seven exoteric and esoteric faculties to the commandment of God, [as in the words of Mary]: '*I have vowed a fast to God*' (19:26). The fifth is almsgiving (*zakāt*), which means donating to the brother in faith [a

67. Ṭūsī comments on the principle of correspondence in the *Sayr wa sulūk* (p.40§31): 'Corresponding to each sensible thing in this world is an intelligible entity in that world, and corresponding to each person here is a spirit there, and corresponding to every manifest thing (*ẓāhir*) here is a hidden one (*bāṭin*) there … That intelligible entity is the source (*maṣdar*) of this sensible one, and this sensible thing is the manifestation (*maẓhar*) of that intelligible one.'

portion] of what God has bestowed upon you and to avoid depriving the needy and poor from their right, in compliance with God's words: '*Practice regular charity, which is the right religion*' (98:5). The sixth is endeavour (*jihād*), which means fighting one's own [carnal] soul (*nafs*) and desires, cutting yourself from everything else apart from God and devoting one's life to the path of the truth, in compliance with: '*Those who strive in God's path with their wealth and life*' (9:20). The seventh is pilgrimage (*ḥajj*), which implies abandoning this perishable world for the sake of the eternal abode (*sarā-yi baqā*), in compliance with: '*What is the life of this world but amusement and play? It is the abode of the Hereafter which is life indeed, if they only knew*' (29:64). And such is the path for the followers of the esoteric aspects (*ṭarīqat-i ahl-i bāṭin*).[68]

[§19] One should abide by the esoteric interpretation of the seven pillars of the religious law, as described here, to be a man of truth (*mard-i ḥaqīqat*). One should be certain that the commandments and prohibitions of the religious law are far easier to perform then the real duties (*takālīf-i ḥaqīqī*), because all of that which is prescribed for a day and night for the man of religious law can be performed in two hours. As for the rest [of day and night], one can engage in whatever is considered important among the worldly tasks, including according to religious law, worshipping God and seeking salvation. The commandments and prohibitions of the truth are more difficult, in the sense that if the man of truth, even for a twinkling of an eye, forgets the real [esoteric aspects of] prayer, fasting and obedience, and becomes negligent, in that period of time, whatever he does or sees will not be for God's sake. Rather, if one drinks a sip of water or eats a morsel of bread aiming to quench thirst and hunger, that sip and morsel, in accordance with the law of truth (*ḥukm-i ḥaqīqat*), will be unlawful to him and he will not be considered a man of truth and esoteric meaning (*mard-i ḥaqīqat wa ahl-i bāṭin*). Rather, the act

68. Ṭūsī's account of the seven pillars here (as also in the *Rawḍa*, pp. 142–150§426–453) is identical to the Fatimid formulation except in respect of *shahādat* which takes the place of *walāyat*. But since Ṭūsī's interpretation of *shahādat* is to know God through the Imam of the time, the two articles are more or less equivalent. On the Fatimid version see al-Qāḍī al-Nu'mān's *Da'ā'im*, vol. 1, pp. 25–99; trans. vol. 1, pp. 18–122.

of obedience that he performs will be futile and he will not be worshipping God, nor will he be granted salvation. Any member of the community (*jamāʿat*) who does not find in himself such a strength, that is, to fulfil the commandments and prohibitions of the truth, it is advisable for him not to abandon obedience to the religious law, or else he would be a loser, both in this world and in the Hereafter (*khasara al-dunyā wa al-ākhira*).

[§20] The one who acts contrary to that mentioned above will be neither a man of religious law nor a man of truth. He undoubtedly will be a deviant (*mulḥid*) and irreligious (*bī-dīn*). May God Almighty grant success to everyone to perform the esoteric and exoteric aspects of obedience? May He bestow steadfastness in obedience to His commands and the guidance of the Imam of the time, following the Qur'ān and the traditions of the Prophet, peace be upon him. May He save us from the whisperings of Satan, the cruelty of tyrannical rulers, and the sudden afflictions and iniquities of the Last Day. May He also grant us a peaceful corner and sufficient provisions [in this world] for the purpose of living.

Āghāz wa anjām
Origin and Destination

In the Name of God the Beneficent, the Merciful

> *Our Lord, Let our hearts not deviate after You have guided us and have bestowed upon us mercy from Your presence, for only You are the Bestower. Our Lord, it is You who will gather mankind together to the Day about which there is no doubt. Truly, God never fails in His promise'* (3:8–9).

[§1] Praise be to the Creator, who is the beginning of all and in whom is the end of all; rather, all is just He. Salutation upon the chosen ones (*barguzīdagān*), who are mankind's guides with respect to the Origin and the Destination, especially upon Muḥammad [the Prophet] and his progeny, peace be upon all of them.

[§2] To begin with, a dear friend beseeched the writer of this admonition, Muḥammad b. Muḥammad al-Ṭūsī, to record a short account of what has been witnessed of the ultimate end of creation by travellers on the path to the Hereafter (*sālikān-i rāh-i ākhirat*), similar to what is written in the Divine Book (*shabīh bi ānchi dar kitāb-i ilāhī mastūr ast*) and has been uttered on the tongue of the prophets and the imams (*awliyā'*), peace be upon all of them, concerning the Resurrection, Paradise, Hell and so forth—not as described by scholars (*ahl-i dānish*), but as witnessed by men of insight (*ahl-i bīnish*).

It was difficult to fulfil his desire because not all that exists is destined for everyone, and not everyone can see what is destined for him, nor can one know all that one sees, nor can one express [in speech] all one knows, and not everyone can write all that he can express. Because, if seeing is by direct vision (*bi'ayn*), knowing can only be a trace (*athar*); if knowledge is conceiving, speaking can only be by informing; and if speech is explicit (*bi taṣrīḥ*), writing can only be by implication and allusion. 'Information cannot be like witnessing, let alone when expressed by hints and allusion.'[69] However, since his mind would get pleasure by this, I could not fail but to assist him in every possible way. Thus, should this treatise fall short of what he expected, he ought not to censure it because its vindication is evident.

[It is hoped] that he and others who read and contemplate [this

69. Text in Arabic.

treatise] will look at it with the eye of forbearance and consider it an obligation to correct the mistakes: '*And my success comes from God; in Him I put my trust, and to Him I look* (11:88). *This is an admonition; so whosoever will, let him take it as a path to his Lord. But you will not, except as God wills, because God is the Knower, the Wise. He admits to his mercy whom He wills, and for the evildoer He has prepared a painful punishment*' (76:29–31).

Our Lord, show us the Truth as truthful and grant us to follow it, and show us the false as falsehood and make provision for us to avoid it. Admit us to your mercy through [mediation] of the chosen one from among your servants. You have power over everything and you are sufficient for us.

[§3] Beginning of the Discourse: The foundation of this treatise is embedded in twenty chapters and the following is the table of contents:

Chapter 12: On the sounding of the Trumpet and transformation of Earth and Heaven.
Chapter 13: On the conditions that occur on the Day of Judgement and the halting of mankind on the plains [of the Resurrection].
Chapter 14: Description of the gates of Paradise and Hell.
Chapter 15: On the tormentors of Hell.
Chapter 16: On the rivers of Paradise and those corresponding to them in Hell.
Chapter 17: On the custodians of Paradise and Hell, and mankind reaching its primordial nature.
Chapter 18: On the Tree of Bliss and the Infernal Tree.
Chapter 19: On the virgins of Paradise.
Chapter 20: On reward and punishment [and God's Justice].

Chapter 1

Description of the path to the Hereafter, its travellers, and the reasons for people's aversion to it, and the calamities attached to that

[§4] Know that the path to the Hereafter is visible, its guides are trustworthy, its signs are apparent and travelling along it is easy, but people are averse to it: '*And how many signs do they pass by in the heavens and the earth, yet they turn their faces away from them*' (12:105). The journey is easy, because it is the same passageway through which people have come. Thus, they have once seen all that is to be seen, and have heard all that is to be heard, but they have forgotten it: '*Truly, We took the covenant of Adam beforehand, but he forgot. Indeed, We did not find him steadfast*' (20:115). In this context [the Qur'ān] states: '*Turn back to your rear, then seek a light*' (57:13). They have been left in forgetfulness because they can neither open the eye through which they have once seen, nor open the ears through which they have once heard. Consequently, their situation reaches the point where '*If you call them to Guidance, they will not listen; you see them looking at you, but they do not see*' (7:198). If one could hear and see what he has heard and seen before, one will recognize. 'The one who looks pays attention, and the one who pays attention recognizes, and the first step in faithfulness (*dīn*) is recognition.'[70]

[§5] And the reasons for aversion are three, as it has been said. The chiefs among the satans are three. One is natural impurities (*shawāʾib-i ṭabīʿat*), like lust, anger and their concomitants such as love for wealth, prestige and other things: '*That is the abode of the Hereafter; it is granted to those who do not seek superiority on earth, nor do they seek corruption, and the end belongs to the righteous*' (28:83). Second is the temptations of habit (*wasāwis-i ʿādat*) such as insinuations of the carnal soul (*taswīlāt-i nafs-i ammāra*), embellishments of unrighteous acts resulting from corrupt fantasies, false imaginations and their concomitants like ugly habits and reprehensible character-traits: '*Say, shall we tell you of those who lose most in respect of their deeds? Those whose efforts have been wasted in this life, yet thinking they do good work*' (18:103–4). The third is conventional laws (*nawāmīs-i amthila*), for example, following devils who are in human attire, and imitation (*taqlīd*) of the ignorant people posing as men of knowledge, responding to the deception and bewilderment of satans from among mankind and the jinn, being deceived by their fraud and cheating: '*O God, show us those among the jinn and mankind who mislead us; we shall place them beneath our feet so that they become the vilest*' (41:29).[71]

---

70. Text in Arabic.

71. In the *Rawḍa* (p. 73§190–192), Ṭūsī describes the three 'satanic chiefs' with variable emphasis. He defines conventional laws, for example, as: '…practices and customs which a truthful master has introduced and imposed on people, as for example, the *qibla* [direction of prayer towards Makah], ritual sacrifices, specifically defined rites, and observances of devotional exercises. All of these come to be so firmly established in their imagination and fantasy, so fixed and set [in their minds], that when another truthful master comes along and seeks to revive for them the spirituality of these commands and prohibitions which they have long since forgotten, and in the course of effecting a more progressive and perfect development, he desires to introduce changes in the practices and rituals of the previous master of truth, they rebel and disobey him and would prefer to kill and burn themselves and their children. Hence they refuse to accept that [renewed] summons.' Ṭūsī also speaks of the 'satanic chiefs' in his *Sharḥ-i*

[§6] The consequence of aversion from the path in this world is blindness and eternal misery in the Hereafter: '*One who is averse from My remembrance will face a hard life and we shall bring him blind to the assembly on the Day of Resurrection. He will say "O God, why have you raised me up blind, while I had sight before?" God will say: "You did the same when My signs came to you; you disregarded them and so you are disregarded today"*.' (20:124–6). Now, what misery may one face above the misery of being ignored before God? Blindness in this context is blindness of the heart: '*Truly, it is not their eyes that are blind, but their hearts in their breasts*' (22:46). Blindness has various degrees of 'seal', 'stamp' and 'stain': '*God has sealed their hearts*' (2:7); '*Rather, God has stamped their hearts because of their infidelity*' (4:155); '*Not at all, but on their hearts He has put a stain*' (83:14). The last one is the ultimate limit of blindness of heart, although it leads to a greater veil: '*Truly, on that Day they will be veiled from their Lord*' (83:15). The greatest of all calamities is that most of those whom people consider as guides are ignorant of the path: '*They only know the outer aspect of life in the world and they are heedless of the Hereafter*' (30:7). Following these people cannot lead except to error: '*If you obey most people on earth, they will lead you away from the path of God. They follow nothing but conjecture and they do nothing but lie*' (6:116).

[§7] Thus, the path for the seeker cannot be anything but holding fast to the rope of God (*ḥabl-i ilāhī*), that is: '*Hold fast all together to the rope of God*' (3:103), and reaching out for the purifying perfect words (*kalimāt-i tāmmāt-i zākiya*), because '*Perfect is the word of your Lord in truth and justice; no one can change His words*' (6:115). '*And enough is your Lord to guide and help*' (25:31).

---

ishārāt wa al-tanbīhāt (vol. 2, p. 1), by quoting Plato that they represent serious obstacles to a clear understanding of philosophy, be it natural or divine.

Chapter 2
On the Origin and the Destination, moving away from primordial nature and going back to it; mention of the Night of Power and the Day of Resurrection

[§8] Primordial nature (*fiṭrat-i ūlā*) is the starting point (*mabdaʾ*) and destination (*maʿād*) is the return to it: '*Set your face towards religion faithfully according to the natural disposition God has established for mankind; there is no change in God's creation, which is the ever-true religion*' (30:30). This is for the reason that at the beginning there was God and nothing else was with Him; then He created mankind out of nothing: '*Indeed, I created you for mercy when you were nothing*' (19:9); and ultimately mankind will become nothing and God alone will remain abiding: '*All that is on earth will perish, and there will remain only the Face of your God, full of majesty and bounty*' (55:26–7). Thus, since mankind's origin is by coming into existence from non-existence, its annihilation after existence will be its destination. Because, coming and going are two opposites and each one can be similar to the other: '*As We originated the first creation, so We will restore it*' (21:104). Therefore, by the decree of the Origin (*ḥukm-i mabdaʾ*), God asks and mankind replies: '*Am I not your Lord? "Yes", they say*' (7:172); and by the decree of Destination, (*ḥukm-i maʿād*), it is God who asks and it is God who replies: '*Who is the Sovereign Lord today? God, the One, the Overpowering,*' (40:16). Since mankind has received its existence from God in the first instance—they did not exist, then they came into existence—so, they will surrender their existence to God: '*Verily, to your Lord is the return*' (86:8); and they will perish: '*Everything will perish except His Face*' (28:88). 'From Him is the origin and to Him will be the return.'[72]

[§9] First, non-existence was the Paradise in which Adam dwelt: '*O Adam, dwell you and your wife in Paradise*' (7:19). Existence after non-existence is to come into this world: '*Fall down from it all of you*' (2:38). The second non-existence, which is annihilation in Unity (*fanāʾ dar tawḥīd*), is the Paradise to which monotheists return: '*Return to your* Lord, content in His good pleasure; enter among His

72. Text in Arabic, alluding to the Qurʾānic verse 2:210.

devotees and enter His Paradise' (89:28–30). Coming from Paradise to earth is heading from perfection to deficiency, and falling from the primordial nature, and inevitably the issuance of existence from the Creator cannot be but in this fashion. Returning to Paradise from this world is heading towards perfection from deficiency and reaching primordial nature, and undoubtedly the return of mankind to the Creator cannot take place except in this manner: '*It is God who originates the creation, then restores it, then unto Him you will be returned*' (30:11). Thus, initially there is falling and descent, followed by rising and ascent. First, the descent of light, then its ascent: '*God is the Light of the heavens and the earth*' (24:25). For this reason [the Qur'ān] speaks of the Origin as night, that is, the Night of Power (*shab-i qadr*), and of the Return as day, that is, the Day of Resurrection (*rūz-i qiyāmat*).

[§10] In the Night of Power '*the angels and the Spirit descend in it by God's permission with all commandments*' (97:4). On the Day of Resurrection, '*the angels and the Spirit ascend unto Him in a day, the span of which is fifty thousand years*' (70:4). As Origin reaches its perfection through Return, similarly night reaches its perfection in day, and day reaches its perfection in month, and month reaches its perfection in year. Therefore, if Origin is the Night of Power, Return will be the Day of Resurrection; and if the Night of Power is compared with month: '*The Night of Power is better than a thousand months, therein descend the angels and the Spirit*' (97:3–4), the Day of Resurrection is compared with year: '*He administers the affair from the heaven unto the earth, then it ascends unto Him in a day, the span of which is a thousand years of your reckoning*' (32:5). From another aspect, if Origin is compared to a day: 'I have blended the clay of mankind for forty mornings with My hands,'[73] the Return may be compared with a year: 'Between the first and the second soundings of the Trumpet, there will be a period of forty years.'[74] If the Night of Power is better than one thousand months: '*The Night of Power is*

73. A *ḥadīth qudsī*, also cited in Ṭūsī, *Akhlāq-i Nāṣirī*, p. 33.

74. A Prophetic tradition reported in *Ṣaḥīḥ Muslim* (Riyadh, 1999), no. [7381] 116–(2940); and M. Bāqir al-Majlisī, *Biḥār al-anwār* (Tehran, 1956–1972), vol. 58, p. 36.

better than a thousand months' (97:3), then the Day of Resurrection is worth fifty thousand years: '*In a day the span of which is fifty thousand years*' (70:4). '*Therefore, hold your patience, a patience of beautiful contentment*' (70:5).

[§11] Moses, who is the man of the Origin and the lord of revelation (*ṣāḥib-i tanzīl*), is lord of the West, where light descends: '*You were not* [O Muḥammad] *on the western side* [of the mountain] *when we decreed the command on Moses* (28:44); and the first book that God Almighty revealed was the Torah. Jesus, who is the man of the Destination (*maʿād*) and lord of esoteric exegesis (*taʾwīl*), is lord of the East, the place where light arises: '*And take note of* [the story of] *Mary in the Book when she withdrew from her family to a place in the East*' (19:16). [Jesus is] '*Knowledge of the Hour*' (43:61) [i.e. of the Resurrection]. Muḥammad, who encompasses both [the realms of East and the West] is, from one aspect an intermediary between the two, and from another aspect apart from both. He encompasses both because he holds a position in the Origin, that is: 'I was a prophet while Adam was between water and clay.'[75] Everything has a substance and the substance of creation is Muḥammad. He also holds a rank in the Destination, because he is the intercessor (*shāfiʿ*) on the Day of Gathering (*rūz-i ḥashr*): 'My intercession is reserved for those who have committed grave sins from among my followers.'[76] As for his being the middle, it is for the reason that from the middle of the earth, to face the Qibla of Moses one has to turn his face towards the west, and to face the Qibla of Jesus one has to turn his face towards the east. To face the Qibla of Muḥammad, one has to face the middle point: 'My Qibla is between the East and the West.' As for him being apart from both: '*He is neither eastern nor western* (24:35). *Verily, in these things there are signs for those who ponder*' (13:3).[77]

---

75. A Prophetic tradition cited in Shahrastānī, *Nihāyat al-aqdām fī ʿilm al-kalām*, ed. and tr. A. Guillaume as *Summa Philosophiae* (London, 1934), Arabic text, p. 494; and Ḥ. Tihrānī, *Imām shināsī* (Tehran, 1405/1984), vol. 1, pp. 222–232.

76. A Prophetic tradition. Majlisī, *Biḥār*, vol. 8, p. 30.

77. A Prophetic tradition. A. J. Wensinck, ed., *al-Muʿjam al-mufahras li-alfāḍ al-ḥadīth al-nabawī* (Leiden, 1965), vol. 5, pp. 259–260.

Chapter 3
Description of the two worlds, and people's status in this world and the Hereafter

[§12] God, the Almighty and Exalted, by virtue of '*He is the First and the Last*' (57:3) owns two worlds: one is the lower world (*dunyā*) and the other is the Hereafter (*ākhirat*), that is, this world and the other world. This world is the Origin (*mabdaʾ*) and the other is the Destination (*maʿād*). Also, by virtue of '*He is the Manifest and the Hidden*' (57:3), He owns two worlds: one is the world of Creation (*ʿālam-i khalq*) and the other is the world of Command (*ʿālam-i amr*). One is the corporeal world (*ʿālam-i mulk*) and the other is the spiritual world (*ʿālam-i malakūt*). One is the hidden world (*ʿālam-i ghayb*) and the other is the manifest world (*ʿālam-i shahādat*). This world is perceptible (*maḥsūs*) and the other is intelligible (*maʿqūl*). Since mankind passes through these worlds, it is incumbent for him to travel from this world to the Hereafter, from the Creation to the Command, from the corporeal to the spiritual, and from the manifest to the hidden. Prophets have been sent, as it is mentioned in the Qurʾān (*guft-i munzal*), to summon mankind from one world to the other. The summons (*daʿwat*) is by informing (*inbāʾ*) and the term 'great news' (*al-nabaʾ al-ʿaẓīm*) [in the Qurʾānic verse] means the other world to which mankind is heading: '*What is that about which they question each other? It is the great news, concerning which they are in disagreement*' (78:1–3).

[§13] In this world, Mankind is in a purgatory (*barzakh*). Purgatory is a dark barrier (*saddī ẓulmānī*) between Origin and Destination: '*And behind them there is purgatory until the Day when they are raised up* (23:100). In this world, people are partly sleeping and some are dead. For the sleeping ones this world is like a dream, and for the dead they are dead, '*without life*' (16:21), '*and you cannot make those who are buried in graves to hear*' (35:22). The one who dies from this life, he will wake up from sleep, because resurrection means waking up. [The Prophet said]: 'When they die, they wake up,'[78] and 'The one who dies,

78. A Prophetic tradition cited in al-Ghazzālī, *Kitāb dhikr al-mawt wa-mā baʿduhu*, tr. T. J. Winter as *The Remembrance of Death and Afterlife* (Cambridge, 1989), p. 124.

his resurrection takes place.'[79] But there are two types of death. One is voluntarily (*irādī*): 'Die before they make you die,'[80] and the other is natural (*ṭabīʿī*): '*Wherever you are, death will catch up with you*' (4:78). The one who dies voluntarily will rise to eternal life: 'Die voluntarily, arise naturally.'[81] But the one who dies naturally will perish eternally: 'Woe to the one who awakens after death.'[82]

[§14] The secret of the Resurrection is a great mystery; the prophets have not been allowed to unveil that secret because they are lords of the religious law (*aṣḥāb-i sharīʿat*). The lords of the Resurrection (*aṣḥāb-i qiyāmat*) are a different group: '*You* [O Muḥammad] *are only a warner, and for every people there is a guide*' (13:7). Muḥammad, May peace of God be upon him, is singled out within proximity to the Resurrection: 'I and the Resurrection (*al-sāʿa*) are like two forefingers.'[83] His position with regard to the Resurrection is thus: '*They will ask you about the Hour "When will the appointed time be?" What can you tell when the answer remains with your Lord? You are but a Warner for the one who is God-fearing*' (79:43–5).

[§15] The Resurrection is the day of reward (*rūz-i thawāb*) and the [period of] religious law (*sharīʿat*) is the day of action. Today there is action without reward; tomorrow there will be reward without action. On the day of the Resurrection, the prophets are witnesses: '*We bring forward from every nation a witness, and bring you forth* [O Muḥammad] *as a witness against them*' (4:41). The lord of the Resurrection is someone else: '*Prophets and witnesses will be brought forward and will judge among them with truth*' (39:69). Religious law (*sharīʿat*) means the path, which is derived from *shārīʿ*; resurrection is destination (*maqṣad*). About the Resurrection the promulgator of the law (*ṣāḥib-i sharʿ*) says: '*I do not know what will be done to you or me*' (46:9).

79. A Prophetic tradition. Majlisī, *Biḥār*, vol. 58, p. 7.

80. A Prophetic tradition also attributed to Jesus and much quoted by the Sufis. See Majlisī, *Biḥār*, vol. 66, p. 317; and L. Badakhshī, *Thamarāt al-quds*, p. 1347.

81. Attributed to Plato by Ṭūsī in *Akhlāq-i Nāṣirī*, p. 188; trans. p. 138.

82. Text in Arabic.

83. A Prophetic tradition. Bukhārī, *Jāmiʿ al-ṣaḥīḥ* (Cairo, 1932), vol. 6, p. 206.

[§16] People are travellers and unless a trace (*athar*) of the destination reaches the traveller, no one will be tempted to travel. No traveller will desire a journey, nor will he travel, until he is aware of the destination. Knowledge of the destination is recognition (*maʿrifat*) and desiring it is love (*maḥabbat*). Thus, unless the knower is a lover, he will not be tempted to travel. Love and recognition are vestiges of attainment (*wuṣūl*), the fulfilment of which is attainment itself, which is called 'the in-gathering' (*ḥashr*): 'Man will be gathered with whomever he loves most.'[84]

[§17] Awareness (*āgāhī*) has various degrees, namely doubt (*ẓann*), knowledge (*ʿilm*) and insight (*ibṣār*). From one aspect, doubt belongs to this world and knowledge to the Hereafter, because in this world: '*Indeed, they are in doubt concerning meeting their Lord*' (41:54), whereas in the Hereafter: '*Certainly He will gather you together on the Day of Resurrection, the indubitable Day*' (4:87). From another aspect, knowledge belongs to this world, but seeing and witnessing belong to the Hereafter: '*Nay, if only you knew with certainty, you would surely see the Hellfire; then, you will perceive it with the eye of certainty, and then you will be questioned about the delight* [of the Hereafter]' (102: 5–8).

[§18] The first vestige of the journey that reaches the travellers is faith (*īmān*). The second vestige is certainty (*īqān*) about the veracity of that faith and its affirmation: '*Verily, this is the certain truth*' (56:85). Certainty is something which they witness in the manifest world (*ʿālam-i shahādat*) and faith is something veiled to them in the hidden world (*ʿālam-i ghayb*): '*Believing in God and the Last Day*' (3:114).[85] Thus, faith belongs to the people of this world: '*They have faith in the unseen*' (2:3), and certainty belongs to the people of the Hereafter '*who have assurance of the Hereafter*' (2:4). Here [the Prophet said:] 'The least that has been bestowed upon you is certainty';[86] this is summoning to faith: '*Believe in your Lord*' (3:193). Certainty also is the

84. Text in Arabic.

85. The order of this sentence has been reversed to convey the sense that the stage of certainty surpasses the simple expression of faith.

86. A Prophetic tradition cited in M. M. Narāqī, *Jāmiʿ al-saʿādāt*, vol. 1, p. 119.

fulfilment and perfection of faith: '*And serve your Lord until certainty comes to you*' (15:99).

[§19] Faith has various stages. In the beginning: *The Arabs said, "we have faith". 'Say, you have no faith, you can only say "we have submitted", because faith has not yet entered your hearts*' (49:14); in the middle: '*And his heart remains firm with faith*' (16:106); and at the end: '*O believers, have faith*' (4:136). Thus, there are [degrees of] faiths, one after another: '*When they guard themselves from evil and believe and do deeds of righteousness, and again guard themselves from evil and believe*' (5:96). Also, faith has conditions: '*But no, by their Lord, they will not believe until they make thee* [the Prophet] *the judge in all disputes between them; then they will find in themselves no resistance against thy verdict, but will submit fully*' (4:65). The first stage is obedience to the command; then, being content with the [divine] ordainment (*qaḍā*), and finally there is submission (*taslīm*).[87]

[§20] Certainty (*īqān*) also has various stages: '*Nay, you will not know; nay, you will not know; nay, if only you knew with certainty, you would surely see the Hellfire; then you will be perceiving it with the eye of certainty, and then you will be questioned about the delight* [of the Hereafter]' (102:3–8). The Hellfire is witnessed after acquiring knowledge of certainty (*ʿilm-i yaqīn*), but witnessing Paradise takes place after obtaining certainty itself (*ʿayn-i yaqīn*). This is for the reason that with knowledge of certainty the veil itself remains, whereas what exists with certainty itself is a trace of the veil.[88]

[§21] Those who doubt (*ahl-i gumān*), assume that Resurrection will take place afar, both in time: '*I doubt the Hour will ever come*' (18:36), and in place: '*And belittle the unseen from a position far off*' (34:53). But the people of certainty are aware that it is near both in time: '*The Hour draws nigh*' (54:1), and in place: '*They were seized from a nearby place*' (34:51); '*They see the Day remote, but We see it near*' (70:6–7). The Prophet, peace be upon him, stretched his hand and fetched a fruit from Paradise, and as long as Ḥāritha did not witness the same,

87. Cf. *Maṭlūb*. §10.
88. Cf. *Tawallā*. §16–18.

he did not approve of him as truly faithful (*mu'min-i ḥaqīqī*). When the Prophet said: 'O Ḥāritha, how did you get up this morning?' 'I got up as a true faithful,' he replied. When the Prophet said: 'There is a reality in every truth, what is the reality of your faith?' Ḥāritha said: 'I saw the dwellers of Paradise visiting each other and the dwellers of Hell hitting one another, and I saw the Throne of my Lord most manifest (*bārizan*).' The Prophet said: 'You are right, stay with it.' Then, the Prophet said to Anas b. Mālik: 'This is a lad whose heart God has illumined with faith.'[89]

Chapter 4
On the place and the time of the Hereafter

[§22] Since the world is imperfect like a child, and for a child nanny and cradle are indispensable, time acts as the world's nanny and place as its cradle; from another aspect time is its father and place its mother. Both time and place are singled out by a trace from their Creator (*mubdi'*), which is their encompassing (*iḥāṭat*) all beings (*kā'ināt*). And the encompassing itself (*'ayn-i iḥāṭat*) belongs to God: '*And God encompasses everything*' (4:126). The encompassing of time, which is a trace of the Creator, is accomplished thus: if one part is the beginning, the other part will be the end. [Similarly], with respect to place, if one part of it is manifest, the other will be hidden. Since [their encompassing] is neither essential (*bi-dhāt*) nor natural (*bi-ṭab'*), none of them is complete by itself. Therefore, the existence of each part of time requires the non-existence of the rest, and the presence of each part of place requires the absence of the rest. Neither past nor future can be named as 'time'. If time has an existence, it is the existence of the present time, which is the shortest possible time, and because of its shortness it has no quantity and scholars call it 'moment'. If place is encompassing, it is the encompassing of the total place and not a part of it, and total place is that which encompasses the heavens and the earth, and the rest of all beings.

89. A Prophetic tradition cited in Kulaynī, *al-Kāfī*, vol. 2, *Kitāb al-īmān*, p. 44.

[§23] The Hereafter is devoid of time and place because it is stripped of deficiency, but when it is described for those who are in time and in place, [the Qurʾān] speaks of it in terms of time and place, sometimes by time and sometimes by place, to render it in a language comprehensible to the people. Reference to time can only be by the shortest possible time like the present time: '*The commandment of the Hour is like the twinkling of an eye or even quicker*' (16:77). Reference to place will be by the most spacious place: '*And a Paradise, the expanse of which is as the width of the heaven and the earth*' (57:21). The act of origination (*ibdāʿ*) is timeless; it is therefore described by the shortest possible time: '*And Our command is but a single act, like the twinkling of an eye*' (54:50). Thus, in this context, origin and return resemble one another; and undoubtedly there is a Hereafter, and its relation to time and space follows the same pattern. As for [the Hereafter] being equated with the shortest possible time, it has been said: 'Certainties are moments',[90] and with respect to the vastness of its place: '*The one whose heart God has opened to Islam is the one with a light from God*' (39:22).

Chapter 5
On the in-gathering of mankind

[§24] Time is the cause of change and place is the cause of multiplicity in an absolute sense. Change and multiplicity are the causes of becoming existing things veiled from one another. In the Resurrection, when time and space are lifted, veils will disappear and mankind, from the first to the last, will be gathered together. Thus, Resurrection is the day of in-gathering (*rūz-i jamʿ*): '*The day you will be gathered for the Day of Assembly*' (64:9). From another aspect, Resurrection is the day of distinction (*rūz-i faṣl*), because this world is the realm of similitudes (*kawn-i mushābahat*), where truth and falsehood look alike, and contenders sit opposite one another. The Hereafter is the realm of distinction (*kawn-i mubāyanat*): On '*the day when the Hour comes, all people will be separated one from another*' (30:14). They will separate truth from falsehood: '*God will make a distinction between the*

90. Text in Arabic.

evil and the good' (8:37). They will rectify the animosity between two contenders. The truth of the truthful and the falsity of the false will be established: '*Those who perish will perish by a clear sign, and those who survive will survive by a clear sign*' (8:42). '*The truth of the truthful and the falsity of the false will be demonstrated*' (8:8). Thus, Resurrection is the Day of Distinction, a distinction that necessitates the above mentioned in-gathering: '*This will be the Day of Distinction; we shall gather you and those before you* (77:38). *Ḥashr* means in-gathering, thus, the Day of Resurrection is the day of in-gathering: '*And we shall gather them all together, not leaving out any one of them*' (18:47).[91]

[§25] But there are various types of in-gatherings. For one group it is like this: '*The day we shall gather the righteous to the Merciful God, like a party presented before a king for honours*' (19:85). For another group it is: '*On the day when God's enemies are gathered together to the Fire*' (41:19). On the whole, everyone's in-gathering will be to what has been the aim of one's endeavour: 'We will gather him with whomever he loves as his friend.'[92] For this reason: '*Assemble the wrongdoers together with their companions*' (37:22); also: '*By God, certainly we*

91. The contrast between the realms of similitude and distinction is an important and recurring theme of the *Rawḍa*. On p. 58§137–138, for example, Ṭūsī writes: 'Moreover, the realm of similitude—in which both the followers of truth and falsehood, the veracious and the liars, the good and the wicked, resemble each other, and where the godless devil is occupied in arbitration and disputation—is absolute Hell. [On the other hand], the realm of distinction where the followers of truth are distinguished from the followers of falsehood, the veracious from the liar and the good from the wicked, and where the godless devil cannot approach the presence of the Most High—is absolute Paradise. The verbal expressions of the scripture pertain to the realm of similitudes and, being endowed [with the particular] characteristics of multiplicity, have the temperament of Hell. On the other hand, esoteric meanings pertain to the realm of distinction and, being endowed [with particular] characteristics of Divine Unity, have the temperament of Paradise. Whoever does not attain to the realm of distinction from the realm of similitudes and does not aspire to find esoteric meanings of the expressions of the Revelation is a denizen of Hell. And whoever attains to the realm of distinction from the realm of similitudes, seeking to find and realizing the esoteric meaning of the exoteric expressions of the revealed scripture is a denizen of Paradise.' See also *Rawḍa*, pp. 74–75§194–195 and pp. 82–83§227.

92. Text in Arabic.

shall gather them and the evil ones together' (19:68), to the extent that: 'If one of you loves a stone, we will gather him with it.'[93]

[§26] When the results of the activity of those who administrate animal purgatories (*muddabbirān-i barāzikh-i ḥayawānī*)—as will be explained later—are formed and exhibited, all those species will be gathered together: '*And when the wild beasts are gathered together*' (81:5). Everyone's in-gathering (*ḥashr*) can only be in his essential form (*ṣūrat-i dhāṭī*). Because there [in the Hereafter], veils are lifted: '*And men will come forth before Almighty God, the One, the Irresistible*' (14:48). For this reason, some people are gathered in a shape, compared to which apes and swine will look beautiful. Also in that world: '*Some are turned into apes and swine and the servants of evil*' (5:63). Notwithstanding that, there are [some] people here in this world who can see the people of the Hereafter. '*Verily, in these things there are signs for those who understand*' (13:4).

Chapter 6
On the circumstances [governing] different classes of people in the Hereafter, and mention of Heaven and Hell

[§27] In this world, those exposed to travelling along the path to the Hereafter are three groups. '*You will be of three kinds: the companions of the right—what about the companions of the right? The companions of the left—what about the companions of the left? And those who are foremost will be the foremost; they will be nearest to God in Gardens of bliss*' (56:7–12). In other words: '*among them there are some who wrong themselves, some who follow the middle course, and some who are foremost in good deeds* (35:32).

[§28] The foremost (*sābiqān*) are the people of unity (*ahl-i waḥdat*), exalted above the path and travel; rather, they themselves are destination for travellers: '*And let not your eye pass away from them in quest of the fineries of this life*' (18:28). Of these are the group that: 'If present, they are not recognized, and if absent they are not missed.'[94]

93. Text in Arabic.
94. Text in Arabic.

The companions of the right (*ahl-i yamīn*) are the good people of the world; they have many ranks corresponding to the degrees of Paradise, but their reward is different: '*And they are of different degrees corresponding to their deeds*' (46:19). The companions of the left (*ahl-i shimāl*) are the evil people of the world; although they have many ranks, corresponding to the descending degrees of Hell, they are all equal in punishment: '*He will say, "Double* [is the penalty] *for everyone, but this you do not understand"*' (7:38). Likewise: '*Truly, that Day all will be equal in punishment*' (37:33).

[§29] All the three groups will pass through Hell: '*Not one of you but will enter it; this is for your Lord a decree which must be accomplished*' (19:71). As for the foremost, 'they shall travel along the path as a flash of lightening'. They cannot avoid Hell: 'We passed through it and its fire was diminished.' These are the words of one of the Imams of the [Prophet's] household, peace be upon all of them, in reply to someone who asked: 'How will you pass through Hell?'[95]

[§30] The companions of the right will be saved from Hellfire and the companions of the left are abandoned there: '*Then we shall rescue those who kept away from evil and leave the evildoers crouching there*' (19:72). The foremost and the companions of the right will reach Paradise, but the perfection of Paradise depends on the foremost: 'Paradise is more eager to receive Salmān than Salmān wishing to enter Paradise.'[96] They do not heed Paradise: '*They do not enter while they have an assurance*' (7:46). They are the people of the Heights (*a'rāf*): '*And on the Heights shall be people who will know everyone by his face*' (7:46). For them, all situations are the same; their condition is described thus: '*Do not grieve for what escapes you, nor rejoice in what has come to you*' (57:23).

95. Attributed to Imam Ja'far al-Ṣādiq. See Thaqafī Tihrānī, *Rawān-i jāwīd* (Tehran, 1399/1978), vol. 3, p. 487.

96. A Prophetic tradition cited in Ḥusayn Mujīb al-Miṣrī, *al-Ṣaḥābī al-jalīl Salmān al-Fārisī 'ind al-'Arab* wa *al-Furs wa al-Turk* (Cairo, 1973), pp. 122–169. Salmān was a Persian companion of the Prophet and much venerated in Shi'ism for his defence of Imam 'Alī's right of succession and his subsequent role in the conversion of Iran. For details, see Louis Massignon, *Salmān Pāk: et les prémices spirituelles de l'Islam Iranien* (Tours, 1934), pp. 16–19.

[§31] The companions of the left are the people of discord (*ahl-i taḍādd*): They are left in contradicting situations which, in this world, are opposite to each other. For example: existence and non-existence, death and life, knowledge and ignorance, power and weakness, pleasure and pain, happiness and misery. This is for the reason that they are left to themselves and on their own they cannot rescue themselves: '*As often as their skins are roasted, we shall exchange them for fresh skins that they may taste the torment*' (4:56). Consequently, they will commute between the two sides of the hot wind (*samūm*) and excessive cold (*zamharīr*) of Hell, and are alternatively punished by each one of them: '*They shall have layers of fire above them and layers of fire below them*' (39:16). Since in this world, they have not submitted to the [divine] command, which is the first stage of faith, and have taken their destiny into their own hands, consequently in the Hereafter they are left constrained: '*Every time they wish to get away from it, they will be forced back into it*' (32:20).

[§32] The companions of the right are the people of gradation (*ahl-i tarattub*). They are always in the state of journeying (*sulūk*), acquiring ranks and perfections one above the other: '*For them are lofty mansions, one above another*' (39:20). They have been saved from the torments facing the people of discord: '*No fear shall come upon them, nor shall they grieve*' (2:62)—grief for things lost and fear of something which yet has not come. Since in this world they have been constrained: '*It is not fitting for a believer, man or woman, when a matter has been decided by God and His Apostle, to have any option about their decision*' (33:36), in the Hereafter they will enjoy absolute free choice: '*wherein they shall have whatever they desire*' (16:31). Thus, by the decree of [divine] justice, everyone will have his share of compulsion and free choice.

[§33] Therefore, if this group exhibit some sort of attachment to either side of discord, that will not be a real discord, and they will not be tormented for it, rather they will be rewarded. Its example is the heat of ginger and the coolness of camphor which are innate (*gharīzī*), unlike the [excessive] warmth and coolness of *samūm* and *zamharīr* which are unnatural (*gharīb*): '*The righteous will drink from a cup mixed with camphor*' (76:5); '*and they will be given to drink from a cup mixed with ginger*' (76:17). Likewise, dispute between the people of gradation is unreal (*majāzī*): '*There they will pass from hand to hand a cup wherein is neither vanity nor cause of sin*' (52:23); consequently: '*We shall remove all the rancour that is in their hearts; as brothers they shall recline on thrones face to face*' (15:47). But dispute between the people of discord is a real one: '*Surely that is true, the dispute between the people of the fire*' (38:64), to the extent that: '*Every time a new group enters, they will curse their sister group* [who preceded them]' (7:38).[97]

[§34] Thus, warmth and coolness which are two opposites, in some cases both cause torment for one group, as in the case of the people of Hell, and in other, one side causes rest and peace for one group: '*O fire! Be coolness and peace*' (21:69)—people on the side of coolness are the God-fearing ones (*muttaqīn*)—and the other side which is hot, causes torment for those who are on the opposite side. It also happens that both of them may cause rest and peace for one group, as noted in the case of ginger and camphor, or cause torment for one group, like the Hellfire. In some cases, fire causes rest for one group, as in the case of the one who asked the distributor of Heaven and Hell (*qasīm al-janna wa al-nār*):[98] 'O distributor of fire! Make me a companion of fire.' He smiled and said: 'I have made you one', and then he turned to those who were present and said: 'He wants to be a companion of the Resurrection.'

[§35] Non-existence also has different types: the non-existence of coercion (*qahr*) which, in the Resurrection, overwhelms both the common people and the elite: '*Everything will perish except His Face*' (28:88); the non-existence of kindness (*luṭf*) which is particular to the people of unity (*ahl-i waḥdat*): 'I will erase the trace of the one who loves Me';[99] and the non-existence of harshness ('*unf*) which is particular to the companions of Hell: '*It neither spares, nor does it leave alone*' (74:28).

---

97. Ṭūsī's threefold categorisation of mankind into the people of discord (*ahl-i taḍādd*), gradation (*tarattub*) and unity (*waḥdat*) is a central motif of the *Rawḍa* (p. 80§219 and n.28p.252), and corresponds to the ignorant (*hamaj*), the pupils (*muta'allim*) and the wise ('*ālim*) of the *Nahj al-balāgha*, p. 496.

98. In his *Akhlāq-i Muḥtashimī*, p. 27, Ṭūsī associates the 'distributor of Heaven and Hell' with Imam 'Alī.

99. Text in Arabic.

Chapter 7
Description of the path

[§36] The *ṣirāṭ* is God's path: '*You do guide man to the straight path*' (42:52). 'The path of God, to whom belongs all that is in the heavens and the earth, is thinner than a hair and sharper than a sword.'[100] It is thin for the reason that if there is the slightest inclination to either side of discord, it will cause perdition: '*And incline not to those who do wrong, or the fire will seize you*' (11:113). It is sharp for the reason that halting on it will also cause perdition: 'The one who halts on it will be cut into two.'[101]

[§37] The people of Hellfire collapse from the path into Hell: '*And those who do not believe in the Hereafter will deviate from the path*' (23:74). Hell is on both sides of the path: 'Left and right are stumbles.'[102] Contrary to those who dwell in the Heights (*a'rāf*), where Paradise is on their right side and Hell on their left side, [for the people of Unity] their left and right is the same: 'Both hands of the Merciful are right hands.'[103]

Chapter 8
On the Scrolls of Deeds, the noble scribes, and the descent of the angels and satans upon good and wicked people

[§38] As long as speech and action remain in the realm of sounds and motions, they do not qualify for permanence and stability. Once they are written down and formed, they become lasting and stable. Everyone who utters a word or performs an act, a trace of it will remain. It is for this reason that the acquisition of a character trait (*malaka*) requires repetition. The existence of that trait facilitates return to those [already learned] words and acts. Otherwise, it

100. A Prophetic tradition cited in Majlisī, *Bihār*, vol. 39, p. 246. In a different context Ṭūsī quotes the same tradition in *Sayr wa sulūk*, p. 38, n. 28.

101. Text in Arabic.

102. Text in Arabic.

103. Text in Arabic. In other words, unlike the people of gradation, those who attain the realm of unity are enabled to transcend all contraries of right and the left, good and evil, and Paradise and Hell.

would not be possible for anyone to learn a science, a craft or a skill, and education of children and perfecting deficient peoples would be of no benefit.

[§39] Thus, the traces of words and actions that remain with human beings are in fact similar to writing and formation of those words and acts. The place of such writings and illustrations is called the 'book of words' (*kitāb-i aqwāl*) and 'scroll of deeds' (*ṣaḥīfa-yi a'māl*). Because when acts and words are recorded, it is [as if] they have been written down, as we will explain later, God the Almighty willing.

[§40] The scribes and illustrators of those words and pictures are the noble scribes (*kirām al-kātibīn*, i.e. recording angels). Those who are stationed on the right side record the good deeds of the companions of the right side (*ahl-i yamīn*), and those on the left side record the bad deeds of the companions of the left side (*ahl-i shimāl*): '*When* [the two angels] *come together, one sitting on the right and one on the left*' (50:17). In a tradition (*khabar*), it is stated that 'Anyone who performs a good act, an angel will be born from that action which brings reward or him, and anyone who performs a bad action, a demon will be born from that action which will torment him.'[104] The glorious Qur'ān itself says: '*Those who say 'Allah is our Lord' and persist upon it, an angel shall descend on them saying, "Fear not, nor be sad, but rejoice in the Paradise that you were promised. We are your friends in the present life and in the Hereafter*"' (41:30–31). Contrary to this: '*Shall I tell you on whom the demons descend? They descend on every guilty impostor*' (26:221–2). Also: '*Whoever blinds himself to the remembrance of the Merciful, We shall assign to him a demon as companion*' (43:36).

[§41] This is what scholars (*ahl-i dānish*) call 'character trait' (*malaka*) and people of insight (*ahl-i bīnish*) call 'angel'; both have the same meaning.[105] If the permanence and stability of such character traits were not taken for granted, the permanence of reward and punishment for acts performed in a short period of time would be

104. Text in Arabic.

105. For Ṭūsī's further discussion of this subject, see *Rawḍa*, pp. 80–81§215–220.

senseless. On the contrary, the tradition which says 'The people of Paradise are in Paradise eternally, and the people of Hell are in Hell eternally as a consequence of their intentions',[106] is recognised and authenticated. Thus, anyone who does a good act, even in proportion to the weight of an atom, or does a bad act, that good or bad action will be noted and pictured in a book which will remain permanently and eternally, and when [the book] is brought before their eyes: '*When the scrolls unfold*' (81:10), those who have neglected will say: '"*What book is this? It leaves out nothing, be it small or great, but takes account of it". They will find all they did in front of themselves, and your God will treat no one with injustice*' (18:49).

[§42] According to the Prophet's traditions, by a simple act of glorification of God (*tasbīḥ*), or doing a meritorious work, a black eyed virgin (*ḥūrī*) will be created whose company will be eternally enjoyed in Paradise. In contrast to this, from the evil acts of sinners, creatures will be created in the Hereafter that cause torment and torture for one group, as it is narrated in the story of the son of Noah: '*His conduct is not righteous*' (11:46), or in the case of the children of Israel: '*And we delivered the children of Israel from a humiliating punishment inflicted by Pharaoh, for he was arrogant and extravagant*' (44:30–31).

[§43] It is reported from the Prophet that 'The infidel is created from the sin of the faithful.'[107] There are many traditions like this, and all of them are based on the premise (*ḥukm*) that '*The Hereafter is real life, if only they knew*' (29:64). Thus, in the eyes of the people of this world, whatever is from behind the veil (*az warā-yi ḥijāb*) will appear lifeless (*ghayr-i ḥayawān*), but when that obstacle and veil is removed it will be life: '*Now we have removed the veil and your sight is keen today*' (50:22). This takes place when one dies from this life, which is real lifelessness, and is revived to the eternal life of the Hereafter,

---

106. There are numerous Qur'ānic verses and Prophetic traditions alluding to the eternality of Paradise and Hell. See Fu'ād ʿAbd al-Bāqī, *al-Muʿjam al-mufahras li-alfāẓ al-Qur'ān al-Karīm* (Beirut, 1945), pp. 236–238; and Ṣadr al-Dīn Shīrāzī, *al-Ḥikma al-mutaʿāliya fī al-aṣfār al-arbaʿa* (Tehran, 1977), vol. 4, pp. 176–178, and vol. 5, p. 293.

107. A Prophetic tradition cited by ʿAbd ʿAhd al-Razzāq Kāshānī in his *Ta'wīlat*, known as *Tafsīr Ibn ʿArabī* (Beirut, 2001), p. 325.

which is dying from this world and seeing things as they really are: '*Can he who was dead, to whom we gave life and a light to walk among people, be like the one who is in the depths of darkness from which he can never get out?*' (6:122). This is indeed the answer to the prayer: 'God show us the things as they really are.'[108]

[§44] Thus, everyone must, when the veils are removed and visions become piercing, read his book and attend to his account: '*And everyman's augury have we fastened to his own neck, and we shall bring forth for him on the Day of Resurrection a book which he will find wide open*: "*Read your book, as your soul will suffice for you today to set an account against you*"' (17:13–14). But if he is a forerunner (*sābiq*) in good deeds or a man of the right side (*ahl-i yamīn*), by the decree 'You die as you live, and rise as you die,' one's book will be handed over to him from his front or right side: '*Then the one whose book is delivered to his right hand, his account will be dealt with ease*' (84:7–8), but if one is among the perverts (*mankūsān*): '*If only you could see how the guilty ones hang their heads before their Lord*' (32:12), or from among the people of the left side (*ahl-i shimāl*), his book will be given to him from his back or left side: '*the one whose book is delivered from behind his back*' (84:10), and '*the one whose book is delivered to his left hand*' (69:25).

Chapter 9
On the Reckoning and the ranks of the people of Reckoning

[§45] On the Day of Reckoning (*rūz-i ḥisāb*) people will be divided into three groups. The first group '*will enter Paradise and receive provision without measure*' (40:40), and they constitute three different classes. First are the foremost (*sābiqān*) and the people of the Height (*aʿrāf*), that is, those who are above reckoning and accountability. It is reported in a tradition (*dar khabar ast*): 'When dervishes are brought to the place of Reckoning (*ḥisābgāh*), the angels will demand their accounts. In reply they say "What have you given us that make us accountable to you?" Then the commandment

108. A Prophetic tradition. See Fakhr al-Dīn Muḥammad b. ʿUmar al-Rāzī, *Tafsīr al-kabīr* (n.d.), vol. 1, p. 126.

of the Exalted Lord will be heard: "They are right, their account is not any concern of yours"."[109] Concerning another group, there is a commandment addressed to the Prophet: '*You are not accountable for them, nor are they in the least accountable for you*' (6:52).[110] The second class are the people of the right side who have not committed any sin: '*And those whom You preserve from sin, that Day they will enjoy Mercy, which will be a great achievement*' (40:9). The third group are those whose books of reckoning are empty of bad deeds.

[§46] The second group of the people of Reckoning (*ahl-i ḥisāb*) are also divided into three classes. The first are those whose book of deeds is empty of any good deed. As for the second, [it is] thus: '*All that they contrive is fruitless and vain is all that they do*' (11:16). And the third class are these: '*We shall turn to the work they have done and make it as scattered dust*' (25:23).

[§47] The third group of the people of Reckoning are those '*who have mixed good deeds with evil acts*' (9:102), and they constitute two classes. There are those who always reckon their accounts [in accordance with]: 'Attend to your account before they do it for you.'[111] Consequently, on the Day of Resurrection '*their account will be dealt with ease*' (84:8). But inevitably, those who have been negligent of the Reckoning, they will face examination: 'And the one whose account is scrutinised will suffer.'[112]

[§48] The Reckoning consists of assembling and adding up the vestiges of good and evil acts performed, so that, by the decree of [God's] justice, everyone is recompensed accordingly. The people of certainty (*muqinān*) are always aware of the sum of their account: 'Reckoning of the faithful will not be deferred to the Day of Resurrection.'[113]

109. I have been unable to establish the source of this saying.

110. The first part of Qur'ānic verse 6:52 identifies this group as '*those who call upon their Lord morning and evening, seeking nothing but His Face*'.

111. A Prophetic tradition cited in Muḥammad Reyshahrī, *Mīzān al-ḥikma* (Tehran, 1998), vol. 1, p. 619.

112. A Prophetic tradition. Majlisī, *Biḥār*, vol. 7, p. 263.

113. Text in Arabic.

Chapter 10
On the weighing of deeds and mention of the Balance

'*The weighing on that Day will be just. Those whose scales are heavy will be saved and those whose scale are light will find their souls in perdition*' (7: 8–9).

[§49] The vestige of every action that necessitates certitude for the mind of its doer (*fā'il*) is more appropriate to be named 'heavy', like heavy loads (*muthaqqilāt*) which prevent vessels from restlessness and turbulence of the sea. And, the vestige of every action that necessitates perplexity of the mind (*taḥayyur-i nafs*) and the pursuit of carnal desire are more appropriate to be called 'light', because with the slightest change that may occur in the air, a light particle flies around and its motion will not be orderly. Contentment (*riḍā*) necessitates certitude of mind, and undoubtedly '*those whose scales are heavy will live in contentment*' (101:6–7).

[§50] Inconsistency in the soul's activity is a vestige of the pursuit of carnal desire (*hawā*) which leads to the blazing fire (*hāwiya*). Consequently, '*The one whose scales are light will have his abode in the bottomless pit; and do you not know what it is? It is a blazing fire*' (101:8–11).

[§51] Also, Iblīs (Satan) was created from fire and Adam from dust: '*You created me from fire and created him from dust*' (7:12). Fire is light and dust is heavy, thus the actions of Iblīs necessitate lightness and those of man necessitate heaviness because '*everyone acts according to his own manner*' (17:84).

[§52] Some have said that the statement 'There is no deity except God (*Lā ilāha illā Allāh*) is a weighing scale.'[114] However, they have added: 'An expression light in speech but heavy on the scale.'

---

114. Attributed to Ḥasan-i Ṣabbāḥ, the founder of the Nizārī Ismaili state in Iran. According to his doctrine of *ta'līm*, the attestation of faith represents a scale comprising both a negation and affirmation: 'On the side of negation (*lā*) are those who rely on their own intellect, and on the side of affirmation (*illā*) are the followers of the truthful teacher, namely the Prophet.' See Shahrastānī, *Kitāb al-milal wa al-niḥal*, Persian trans., Jalālī Nā'īnī (Tehran, 1321 Sh./1942), p. 216; and Hodgson, *The Order of Assassins*, pp. 50–57 and 332.

Notwithstanding that, for some weighing and the scale are one and the same thing. The sign that this dictum is a weighing scale is that it has existence on one tray and non-existence on the other, and the particle of negation [*illā*] facing existence and non-existence acts as a pointer (*shāhīn*) upon which both trays are balanced. It faces non-existence from one side and existence from another. The word [*illā*] separates Muslims from infidels, and the people of Paradise from the people of Hell. [Consequently], 'The one who says *Lā ilāha illā Allāh* will enter Paradise'.[115]

Chapter 11
On the rolling-up of the Heavens

[§53] God's Speech is one thing and His Book is a different thing. Speech belongs to the realm of the Command (*amr*) and book belongs to the realm of Creation (*khalq*): '*His command, when He wills a thing, is to say "Be", and it is*' (36:82). The realm of the Command is devoid of contradiction (*taḍādd*) and multiplicity (*takaththur*): '*And Our Command is but one*' (54:50). But the realm of Creation involves contradiction and gradation (*tarattub*): '*Not a thing moist or dry but is in a manifest Book*' (6:59).

[§54] As speech contains signs (*āyāt*): '*These are the signs of God we recite to you in truth*' (2:252), the book also contains signs: '*Those are the signs of the manifest Book*' (28:2). When speech is written down (*mushakhkhaṣ shawad*) it will be a book, similar to the command when it is carried out will be action: '"*Be*', *and it is*' (36:82). Thus, the landscape (*ṣaḥīfa*) of the created world (*ʿālam-i khalq*) is God's Book, Exalted be His Majesty, and His signs are the very things as they are (*aʿyān-i mawjūdāt*): '*In the alteration of night and day, and what God has created in the heavens and the earth, surely there are signs for people who are God fearing*' (10:6). In that Book, all signs are visible and registered, so that people may arrive at the truth by contemplating the signs related to God's action (*āyāt-i fiʿlī*) pertaining to nature (*āfāq*), and listening to verbal signs (*āyāt-i*

115. A Prophetic tradition cited in Āmulī's commentary on *Āghāz wa anjām*, pp. 151–152.

qawlī) visible in the souls (*anfus*): '*We shall show them Our signs in nature and in their own souls, until it become clear to them that it is the truth*' (41: 54).

[§55] As long as man is subject to time and space, they [the angels], will read and show him the signs, one sign after another, one day after another, one situation after another as he witnesses: '*And remind them of the Days of God. Surely therein are signs*' (14:5), like someone who reads a letter, one line after another and one word after another. Once his eye of insight is opened, with the antimony of guidance—as it is said in relation to the adherents of Resurrection—he will leave the realm of Creation (*'ālam-i khalq*) and will arrive in the realm of the Command (*'ālam-i amr*), namely, the abode which was his origin. He will become cognizant of the entire Book instantly, like someone having a rolled-up scroll containing many lines and words in front of him: '*The day when We shall roll up heaven like a scroll rolled-up for books*' (21:104); '*and the heavens shall be rolled-up in His right hand*' (39:67). He does not say his left hand to make it known that the people of the left side will not have a share in the rolling up of the heavens. If, by himself, he is not able to read, nor does he listen to what is read to him, his situation is described thus: '*He hears the signs of God recited to him, yet continues in his arrogance as though he heard them not. Give him the news of a painful chastisement*' (45:8). In relation to hearing, seeing, speech and book, there are many secrets, the mention of which is not possible in a short treatise like this.[116]

Chapter 12
On the sounding of the Trumpet and transformation of Earth and Heaven

[§56] There are two soundings of the Trumpet (*nafkha-yi ṣūr*) on the Day of Resurrection (*qiyāmat*). The first is about causing death for anything having life, be it a dweller of earth or heaven,

116. Ṭūsī devotes an entire chapter on language, speech and hearing in *Rawḍa*, pp. 133–136, §390–401.

that is, the followers of the exoterics of revelation (*ẓāhir-i tanzīl*) or the esoteric interpretation (*bāṭin-i ta'wīl*) Here, we attempt an interpretation from both the physical (*maḥsūs*) and intellectual (*maʿqūl*) points of view: '*For the Trumpet will be sounded, when all that are in the heavens and on the earth will swoon, except whom God wishes*' (39: 68).

[§57] Their death signifies the exposure of defective beliefs (*maqālāt*) and refutation of what they have published (*nashr*) of their religious tenets (*diyānāt*), so that by the futility of one's knowledge and insight, the truth of [the Qur'ānic words] are fully known and realized: '*Surely you, and that which you worship apart from God, are fuel for Hell; you shall go down to it*' (21:98); and: '*When the word is fulfilled against them, We shall bring forth a beast from the earth to speak to them, because mankind did not believe in Our signs*' (27:82).

[§58] The second sounding will be for revival after death and one's awakening from the sleep of ignorance:[117] '*Then it will sound again and that will be the Resurrection they will witness*' (39:68). That will be the final rising (*qiyām-i qiyāmat*) and the Day of Resurrection is called the 'Rising' (*baʿth*): '*Then on the Day of Resurrection you will surely be raised up*' (23:16); Thereafter, there will only be reward and punishment. Notwithstanding that, there are people in this world who are united with their Hereafter: 'Even if the veils were

117. Cf. *Rawḍa* (p. 92§263–264): '...regarding the resurrection of the spirits (*ḥashr-i arwāḥ*), this human body is like a tomb for the soul. Every soul whose inclination and yearning is for body and the physical world (*ʿālam-i ṭabīʿat*), and which is imprisoned in the hands of the devils of lust and anger, being heedless of Almighty God's Command, has in reality died the death of ignorance. Such a soul has already fallen into the tomb of its tenebrous body and fallen prey to hellish passions and desires. The resurrection of such folk will be the resurrection of their souls which have died the death of ignorance, [as has been said]: They lie fast asleep, entombed in their bodies, darkened by infernal passions and desires. Then, when the Trumpet of the [Day of] Resurrection (*ṣūr-i qiyāmat*) is blown, that is, when the call of the summons of the Resurrector (*daʿwat-i qā'im*) is given, they will be resurrected from the tomb of the flesh, that is, they will be roused and revived by the spirit of faith: '*Answer God and His Prophet when He summons you to that which gives you life*' (8:24).

removed, my certainty will not increase.'[118] They do not need [to wait for Hereafter]: '*Now we have removed the veil and your sight is sharp*' (50:22). Thus, for them action and reward will be one and the same thing: 'I worship God not out of love or fear, but because He is worthy of being worshipped.'[119] Thus, they do not wait for the Resurrection (*qiyāmat*), the Rising (*ba'th*) or reward (*thawāb*).

[§59] For others than these, it will be disclosed in the second creation (*nash'at-i thāniya*) that their existence was non-existence and their non-existence has been existence; possessing a self has been selflessness and their selflessness has been possessing a self; and having an attribute was the lack of attribute and attributelessness was having an attribute. Then they will realize that the exoteric of things was not as they had assumed, nor the esoteric and reality of things were esoteric and reality as they had assumed. Further, by the removal of exoteric and esoteric veils they will realize the reality of things, and that the earth was not what they assumed to be in the first creation, nor the sky as they knew it: '*The Day when the earth will be changed to a different earth, and so will be the Heavens, and [men] will come forth unto God, the One, the Mighty*' (14:48).

Chapter 13
On the conditions that occur on the Day of Judgement and the halting of mankind on the plains [of the Resurrection]

[§60] In the making of this world, the sun is the effuser of universal light (*anwār-i kullī*), and the moon receives light from the sun and in its absence imparts that light to what is beneath it. The stars are the source for the effusion of partial lights (*anwār-i juzwī*). Thus, when the Light of all lights (*nūr al-anwār*) will become manifest, stars will fail to exist: '*When the stars are scattered*' (82:2); the moon will disappear: '*When the moon is eclipsed*' (75:8), and the effused joins the effuser: '*And the sun and the moon are brought together*' (75:9). When partial and universal lights are united, there remains neither effusion

118. Attributed to Imam 'Alī, in Āmidī, *Ghurar al-ḥikam wa durar al-kilam* (Ṣaydā, Lebanon 1931), vol. 1, p. 119.

119. Attributed to Imam 'Alī. Majlisī, *Biḥār*, vol. 1, p. 239.

(*ifāḍat*) nor receptivity (*istifāḍat*): '*When the sun is darkened*' (81:1), and '*They will perceive neither* [the burning heat of] *the sun nor severe cold* [of the moon] (*zamharīr*) (76:13).

[§61] At first, mountains that cause unevenness in the path of attainment (*ṭuruq-i wuṣūl*), and suffering and fatigue of the journey (*sulūk*), will be turned into '*carded wool*' (101:5), and at the end they will be annihilated completely: '*They will ask you about the mountains; say: "My Lord will scatter them far and wide. Then He will level the earth and you will see neither curve nor crookedness there*"' (20:105–7), that is, [neither] anthropomorphism (*tashbīh*), [nor] anti-anthropomorphism (*tanzīh*).

[§62] And the oceans—passing through them and reaching the shore of safety is only possible by ships navigating by shining stars—are removed: '*When the oceans boil over*' (81:6). Consequently, sea and land, up and down, sky and earth, will all be levelled, and mankind will arrive at the plain of the Resurrection (*ʿaraṣāt*): '*When they will be fully awakened*' (79:14). Veils, coarse or subtle, will be removed from the front of the people of the purgatories (*ahl-i barāzikh*): '*When the graves are overturned*' (82:4), and secrets will be unveiled for them: '*and halt them for questioning*' (37:24).

[§63] Those saved from the confinement of the purgatory will move to the presence of God (*bārgāh-i rubūbiyyat*): '*Then, from the graves they will come forth unto their Lord*' (36:52). Poisons, fangs, nails and horns will be taken away from reptiles, predators and beasts, thus breaking the severity of the two sides of discord (*taḍādd*). The poison will be removed from the viper, the claws from the wolf and horns from the ram: '*They will perceive neither* [the burning heat of] *the sun nor severe cold* [of the moon] (*zamharīr*) (76:13).

[§64] Death, which causes the annihilation of all creatures on both sides of the discord (*taḍādd*), will be killed in the form of a black and white ram (*kabshī amlaḥ*) between Paradise and Hell. By the killing of death, which is annihilation of non-existence, absolute existence which is the eternal life will become manifest. Hell in the shape of a camel will be summoned to the planes of Resurrection: '*and Hell is brought forth on that Day*' (89:23) in a way that those with eyes may see: '*and Hell will be exhibited for all to see*' (79:36). Trembling from looking at Hell, all parts of creation will realize their non-existence: 'The camel broke loose in such a way that, if God had not shackled it, the heaven and earth would have been burnt.'[120]

Chapter 14
Description of the gates of Paradise and Hell

[§65] The animal faculties (*mashā'ir-i ḥayawānī*), through which the elements of the physical world are perceived, are seven. Five are apparent (*ẓāhir*), that is, the five sense perceptions, and the other two are hidden (*bāṭin*) faculties, namely imagination (*khayāl*) and estimation (*wahm*).[121] Imagination perceives shapes and estimation perceives meanings. Thinking (*mufakkira*), memory (*ḥāfiẓa*) and recollection (*dhākira*) are not considered faculties; rather, they are supporters (*a'wān*). For, a soul that pursues vain desire and makes the intellect subservient to vanity: '*Have you seen the one who takes his vain desires as his god?*' (45:23), each of these faculties will become a cause for annihilation (*halāk*): '*and God, has knowingly sent him astray*' (45:23). The state of such a soul can be described as: '*The one who transgressed and preferred the life of the world, surely blazing fire will be his abode*' (79:37–39). Therefore, each faculty will be a gate to Hell: '*For it has seven gates leading to it, and each gate receives a part of them*' (15:44).

[§66] If the intellect that perceives the spiritual world (*ālam-i malakūt*) and acts as the head of the above-mentioned faculties is obeyed unconditionally (*ra'īsī muṭā' bāshad*), then through each faculty, one can comprehend a specific domain of the physical world

120. Attributed to Imam Ja'far al-Ṣādiq, cited in Majlisī, *Biḥār*, vol. 3, p. 391; for a different version see Āmulī's commentary on *Āghāz*, p. 181.

121. Cf. *Rawḍa* (pp. 30–46§38–101) for Ṭūsī's analysis of human faculties. With reference to imagination and estimation, for example, he writes: 'The lower aspect of imagination is sense and its higher aspect is estimation. The lower aspect of estimation is imagination and its higher aspect is soul. The lower aspect of soul is estimation and its higher aspect is intellect. The lower aspect of intellect is the soul and its higher aspect is the [Divine] Command.'

(*kitāb-i khalqī*) assigned to that faculty. Also through the intellect, if one responds to the divine words revealed from the realm of the Command (*'ālam-i amrī*)—contrary to [those who say]: '*If we had only listened or understood, we would not have become the inhabitants of Hell*' (67:10)—each one of the above faculties, that is, seven plus intellect which makes it eight, will be like a gate to Paradise: '*As for him who is mindful of the rank of his Lord, and restrains his soul from vain desires, then Paradise will be his abode*' (79:40–41).

Chapter 15
On the tormentors of Hell

[§67] The administrators (*muddabbirān*) of the affairs of the upper purgatories (*barāzikh-i 'ulwī*), as described [in the Qur'ān]: '*Those gliding along, those pressing forward as in a race, and those who govern the affairs*' (79:4–6), are seven stars moving in the twelve signs of the Zodiac. The sum of seven and twelve is nineteen.[122] The conductors (*mubāshirān*) of the affairs of the lower purgatories (*barāzikh-i suflī*) are also nineteen. There are seven sources for the vegetative faculties (*mabda'-i quwā-yi ḥayawānī*), that is: three fundamentals (*aṣl*), namely growth (*nāmiya*), form-giving (*muṣawwira*) and generative (*muwallida*); and four derivatives, namely absorption (*jādhiba*), retention (*māsika*), digestion (*hāḍima*) and repulsion (*dāfi'a*). The sources for the animal faculties are also twelve. Ten of them deal with sensation, namely the five apparent senses and the five that are hidden, namely the *sensus communis* (*ḥiss-i mushtarak*), estimation (*wahm*), imagination (*mutakhayyila*), memory (*ḥāfiẓa*) and recollection (*dhākira*). The other two are sources for movement (*mabādī-yi taḥrīk*): one is the faculty of absorption (*quwwat-i jadhb*), and the other is the faculty of repulsion (*quwwat-i daf'*), the sum of which is nineteen.

[§68] Thus, so long as man is imprisoned in the confinement of the lower world, they are detainees of the imprint of these nineteen heavenly and nineteen earthly administrators If one could not pass through this abode (*manzil*), inevitably [as stated in the tradition]:

122. A reference to Qur'ān 74: 30: '*Over it are nineteen*'.

'You die as you live and rise as you die,'[123] he will fall from worldly confinement (*sijn*) to the confinement of Hell (*sijjīn*). There he will be tormented by the Lord of Hell (*mālik-i jihannam*) through these nineteen tormentors (*zabāniya*), as a result of his connection with one of the two groups of nineteen, or as has been said, they have become attached to him: [The tormentors of Hell] *are nineteen* (74:30).

[§69] Unless one walks by the Straight Path: '*This is My path, the straight path; so follow it and do not follow [other] paths, lest they distance you from God's path*' (6:153), and with the guiding light of the Lord of Resurrection (*hādī-yi qiyāmat*) arrives at the abode of peace (*dār al-salām*), one cannot be saved from these nineteen tormentors: '*God puts forth a parable of a man who has for his masters several quarrelling partners, and a man depending wholly on one person. Are these two equal in status? God be praised! But most people do not know*' (39:29).

Chapter 16
On the rivers of Paradise and those corresponding to them in Hell

[§70] Water is the substance (*mādda*) of life for all types of plants and animals: '*and We made from water everything living*' (21:30), like sermons and advice that benefit the general public. But a kind of it is bitter, some is polluted and some pure. The best water is the pure one.[124]

[§71] Milk is the source of growth for various kinds of animals. It is more exclusive than water because plants and some kind of animals cannot consume it. Milk in particular is food for some kinds of animal in their infancy. It is like the elementary, exoteric knowledge which is suitable for guiding beginners. A type of milk is transformed (*mustaḥīl*), another is changed in flavour (*mutaghayyir*) and some

123. A Prophetic tradition cited by M. Ḥusayn Ṭabāṭaba'ī in *al-Mīzān fī tafsīr al-Qur'ān* (Tehran, 1974), vol. 1, p. 89; and Ḥāfiẓ Rajab Bursī, *Mashāriq al-anwār al-yaqīn fī ḥaqā'iq asrār Amīr al-Mu'minīn* (Tehran, n.d.), p. 200. See also §13 above for similar traditions.

124. Ref. Qur'ān 47: 15.

remains unchanged. The best kind of milk is the type whose flavour has not changed.

[§72] Honey is more exclusive than milk. It is food for some kind of animals and, under certain circumstances, it is medicine for others. It is not suitable for all temperaments and conditions. It is like the [spiritual] realities that obscure issues of knowledge, which only the elite of the elites (*khāṣṣ al-khawāṣṣ*) and scholars can understand. Of honey too, one kind is turbid (*kadir*), some is average (*muṭawassiṭ*) and some refined (*muṣaffā*), and the best kind is the refined one.

[§73] Wine is more exclusive than honey because it is particular to mankind. Among humans, under certain conditions, it is unlawful (*ḥarām*) for the people of this world and an abomination (*rijs*), but it is clean (*ṭahūr*) and lawful (*ḥalāl*) for the inhabitants of Paradise. Of wine too, one kind is harmful (*mu'aḍḍī*), some is average and some pleasant (*mulidhdh*). Its best kind is the clean and pleasant one.

[§74] Thus, water quenches thirst, milk removes deficiency, honey cures sickness and wine causes freedom from grief, and because the people of Paradise are the people of perfection, their benefit from all four is total and in the most perfect manner. This is for the reason that, whatever the imperfects enjoy from, they are also beneficial to the perfect ones (*kāmil*), but its reverse is not correct: '*A similitude of Paradise which the God-fearing are promised is of rivers of water incorruptible, rivers of milk unchanging in flavour, and rivers of wine delighting to the drinkers, and rivers too of honey purified; and therein or them is every kind of fruit*' (47:15).[125]

125. Cf. Ṭūsī's esoteric exegesis of the 'rivers of Paradise' in *Rawḍa* (p. 151§454): 'According to the literal revelation (*tanzīl*), the four streams of Paradise consist of water, milk, honey and wine. According to spiritual exegesis (*ta'wīl*), they stand for four kinds of knowledge as befitting the varying capacities of human intellects. Thus, water symbolizes immediate and self-evident knowledge (*'ilm-i badīhī*) common to all men which can be communicated and is accessible to everyone. Milk symbolizes instructional knowledge (*'ilm-i naẓarī*) which is reserved for 'children', that is, those of weak intelligence. Honey symbolizes authoritative knowledge (*'ilm-i ta'līmī*) which can only be imparted to one kind of people, namely those who have progressed beyond the realm of personal opinion (*kawn-i naẓar*) and turned from degeneracy to rectitude. Wine symbolizes divinely inspired knowledge (*'ilm-i ta'yīdī*) which results from the disclosure of spiritual realities. This type of

[§75] But in the eyes of the people of this world, the fruits of Paradise appear alike (*mutashābih numāyad*), and the case is the same for other things beneath each of them. Because here truth and falsehood are ambiguous: '*They are given things that are similar*' (2:25). In Hell, corresponding to the four mentioned rivers, there are four rivers of Ḥamīm, Ghaslīn, Qaṭrān and Muhl:[126] '*And such are the signs we relate to mankind, but no one will grasp their meaning except the wise*' (29:43).

Chapter 17
On the custodians of Paradise and Hell, and mankind reaching its primordial nature

[§76] At the primordial creation (*nash'at-i ūlā*), initially existence was bestowed upon mankind, then they were given knowledge, then power and finally volition. Because in the beginning, for a while man existed in the form of seed, sperm, clotted blood, bone and flesh, and then he became alive and conscious (*khabar dār*): '*Has there not passed on mankind a period of time, when he was not worth mentioning?*' (76:1). For a while he was living, and then the faculties of movement and rationality (*nuṭq*) appeared in him. For a while he possessed movement, and then the faculty of discrimination between beneficial and harmful was actualized in him, and it was after that that he came to be willing to seek the beneficial and loath the harmful.

[§77] Since Destination (*ma'ād*) is return to primordial nature (*fiṭrat-i awwal*), it is essential therefore that all these [acquired] attributes

knowledge is suitable only for persons of a sound temperament who, having turned away from a degenerate state to a condition of rectitude, move from rectitude to Divine Unity. With the latter type of persons there is no need for one to engage in dissimulation (*taqiyya*) and it is improper to do so.'

126. Muhammad Asad, in his translation of the Qur'ān, renders the names of the four rivers of Hell as 'burning despair' for Ḥamīm (p. 182, n. 62), 'filth' for Ghaslīn (p. 89, n. 21), 'black pitch garment' for Qaṭrān (p. 380, n. 65) and Muhl in the verse 29:18 as 'molten lead'. Yusuf Ali has 'boiling water' for Ḥamīm, 'corruption from the washing of wounds' for Ghaslīn, 'garments of liquid pitch' for Qaṭrān, and 'melted brass' for Muhl.

melt away in him in the reverse order. Thus, first of all, one's volition must be submerged and annihilated in the will of the Absolute One (*wāḥid-i muṭlaq*) who is the Universal Originator (*mūjid-i kull*), to the extent that there does not remain any volition of his own. And because existence follows the will of the Absolute One, Exalted be His mention, whatever the outcome, it will correspond to the will of God. This is the rank of contentment (*riḍā*) and the holder of this rank will always be in Paradise: '*Therein they shall have whatever they desire, and We have yet much more*' (50:35). For this reason the custodian of Paradise is called the 'contented one' (*riḍwān*), and until one reaches this rank, one cannot enjoy the delights of Paradise: '*and the greatest bliss is contentment from God*' (9:72).

[§78] After this, one's power must be annihilated in God's exalted power, to the degree that one may not find his own power to be apart from that of God. This is called the stage of trust (*martaba-yi tawakkul*): '*And whosoever puts his trust in God, He shall suffice him. God attains His purpose. Truly, God has ordained a measure for everything* (65:3).

[§79] After this, one's knowledge must be annihilated in God's knowledge, to the extent that one may know nothing on his own. This is the stage of submission (*taslīm*): '*and submit with the fullest conviction*' (4:65).

[§80] After this, one's existence must annihilate in God's existence, to the extent that one should be nothing on his own. This is the rank of the people of unity (*maqām-i ahl-i waḥdat*): '*They are the ones whom God has blessed among the Apostles*' (19:58).

[§81] If the traveller (*sālik*) does not proceed along this path, and follows his own volition, his volition will require diverse desires of untruth which: '*If God had to accord with their desires, heaven and earth and everything therein would have become corrupt*' (23:71). Thus, one will not be restrained from his own passions: '*and if a barrier* [is not established] *between them and what they desire*' (34:54), they will face God's anger: '*Is the one who obeys God's desire the same as the one who faces His wrath?*' (3:162). His passion shall lead him to Hell; he will be entangled in shackles and chains of total discontent (*nāmurādī*). Discontent is the attribute of slaves (*mamālīk*), and for this reason the custodian of Hell is called the 'owner' (*mālik*).

[§82] After this, corresponding to the ascending rank of trust (*tawwakul*), there is the descending rank of desertion (*khidhlān*): '*And if God deserts you, who else can help you after Him?*' (3:160). Corresponding to the ascending rank of submission (*taslīm*), there is the descending rank of disgrace (*hawān*): '*And the one disgraced by God, there is none to honour him*' (22:18). Corresponding to the ascending rank of unity (*waḥdat*), there is the descending rank of curse (*la'nat*): '*They are cursed by God and the cursers*' (2:159). Thus, just as annihilation in God's power, knowledge and existence for the first group necessitated limitless power, essential knowledge and eternal existence: '*That is a mighty triumph*' (9:90), nourishment (*istimdād*) of the second group from the above mentioned attributes will necessitate limitless weakness, total ignorance and eternal non-existence: '*That is the supreme disgrace*' (9:63).

Chapter 18
On the Tree of Bliss and the Infernal Tree

[§83] For mankind, knowledge, power and volition, which are the source for people's actions, are three different attributes, whereas for God, all of them are one and the same thing. But from different perspectives related to human intelligence, they appear to be three different attributes. Take the example of our own minds (*ḍamāyir*) which are related to the realm of the Command. If we comprehend a rational non-perceptual form, that form because of being conceived by us, is known to us and we have knowledge of it; and because we gave existence to it, it is within our power and we have control over it; and because as long as we do not exercise a volition, it does not appear in our comprehension, we have will over it and it is subject to our volition. Thus, our knowledge, power and volition would be one and the same thing, and as such our knowledge, power and volition are united. In relation to God Almighty's knowledge, power and volition, the entire existence follows the same pattern, and for Him all the three attributes are united, or rather, they are one.

[§84] The same applies to the one who is knowledgeable through God's knowledge, powerful through His power, and willing through His volition, as we stated in relation to the people of Paradise and as mentioned in the Prophetic tradition: 'I will be His ear by which He hears, and His eye by which He sees',[127] which implies the same, that is, 'Obey Me, I will make you like Myself, and there is nothing like Me, and God is All-seeing and All-hearing.'[128] Thus, whatever one may desire will materialize instantly, that is, desiring something and its fulfilment will be one and the same thing. This is the meaning of the Tree of Bliss (*dirakht-i ṭūbā*)[129] in Paradise, because, instantly, whatever the people of Paradise wish, it will be fulfilled through that Tree and will be presented to them: '*Joy is for them and their journey ends in bliss*' (13:29).

[§85] Correspondingly, for people who require these three attributes in multiplicity, in relation to each one of the above mentioned attributes, a kind of frustration and torment comes into existence: '*Depart into the threefold shade, where there is no relief or shelter from the flames*' (77:30–31). Thus, for them, instead of the Tree of Bliss, there is the Infernal Tree (*dirakht-i zaqqūm*): '*It is a tree that shoots out of the bottom of Hellfire; its sprouts are like the heads of devils*' (37:64–45). 'Sprouting' (*ṭil'*) is the beginning of germination of seed which causes the growth of a tree. 'Heads of devils' refers to partial

---

127. A Prophetic tradition. Kulaynī, *al-Kāfī*, vol. 2, p. 236.

128. Quoted as a *ḥadīth qudsī*' in Āmulī's commentary on *Āghāz*, pp. 222–223.

129. It is generally accepted that the word *ṭūbā*, translated here as 'Tree of Bliss', refers to a tree in Paradise with a branch in every chamber, producing the most delicious and aromatic fruit for its residence. The term appears once in the Qur'ān (13:29) and is translated by Yusuf Ali as 'blessedness' and by Muhammad Asad as 'happiness'. The tree is often mentioned in Persian poetry, with varying meaning depending on the context. Nāṣir-i Khusraw in his *Dīwān*, ed. Mujtabā Mīnuwī and Mahdī Muḥaqqiq (Tehran, 1974), p. 479, for example, compares his poems to the 'tree of bliss' (*dirakht-i ṭūbā*):

درختی ساختم مانند طوبی خرّم و زیبا
که هر لفظیش دیناریست و هر معنیش خرمائی

'I have produced a tree similar to the 'Tree of Bliss / each word of it a gold coin, and each meanings a sweet date.'

desires (*ahwā'-i juzwiyya*): 'The devil moves among human beings like blood in the veins.'[130] Their heads which are the source of carnal desires are the shoots of the branches of such a tree, which is the source of Hellfire.

Chapter 19
On the virgins of Paradise

[§86] When, with the antimony of God's grace (*kuḥl-i tawfīq*), one's eye of insight is opened and, like [the Prophet] Abraham, one becomes capable of observing the spirituality of both worlds: '*So We showed Abraham the power of the heaven and the earth so that he might be among the men of certitude*' (6:75), then, through the light of emanation, one will witness visitors from the exalted realm (*wāridān-i ḥaḍrat-i 'izzat*) that manifest themselves in each and every particle of existence from beyond the veil of the hidden world (*parda-yi ghayb*). And inevitably, as mentioned earlier, they are witnessed in the most tantalizing form from among the worldly shapes. Similar to what is mentioned in the story of Mary: '[*Then We sent Our Spirit*] *and it appeared to her in the likeness of a perfect man*' (19:17).

[§87] And because the joy of witnessing (*mushāhada*) that delight is impossible except through a vestige from the emanation of the realm of Unity (*atharī az ālam-i waḥdat*), necessitating the union (*izdawāj*) between essence and form (*dhāt wa ṣūrat*), leading to unification between them, consequently a marriage will take place between him and each one of those forms, that is, the virgins of Paradise: '*and We shall wed them to the wide-eyed maidens of Paradise*' (44:54); and since the faces of these virgins are well protected from the eyes of strangers and the people of discord (*ahl-i taḍādd*): '*wide-eyed maidens cloistered in pavilions*' (55:74), by the decree that, strangers, be it from the realm of multiplicity (*takaththur*)—that is, those abandoned in the externalities (*ẓāhir*) of the physical world, or those veiled by the mysteries (*baṭin*) of the spiritual world—cannot enjoy such a marriage: '*They are touched neither by man nor jinn*'

130. A Prophetic tradition. Suyūṭī, *al-Jāmi' al-ṣaqīr*, vol. 1, p. 82.

(55:74). And because the return of that state, each and every time, is more pleasant than before, like a beloved who has been found after a painful search, novelty and freshness of that joy is renewed again, each and every time.[131]

Chapter 20
On reward and punishment [and God's Justice]

[§88] Reward belongs to God's grace (*faḍl*) and punishment belongs to His justice (*ʿadl*). For this reason: '*Whosoever performs a good deed, he shall receive better than it*' (27:89); and '*Whosoever has done an evil deed, he shall be recompensed only for that which has been done*' (28:84). Also: '*Whosoever has done a good deed shall have ten times of the like*' (6:160). In another place: '*The parable of those who spend their wealth in the way of God is that of a grain which grows seven ears, and each ear has a hundred grains. God multiplies unto whom He wills*' (2:261).

[§89] But there are people who belong to the category of [God's] grace: '*God will change their evil deeds into good deeds*' (25:70), and in the opposite side are those '*whose deeds have failed*' (2:217). Also, there are people who belong to the category of [God's] justice: '*Then whosoever has done an atom's weight of good shall see it, and whosoever has done an atom's weight of evil shall see it*' (99:7–8), and in the opposite side there are those in relation to whom [God says]: '*Assuredly in the Hereafter they will be the greatest losers*' (11:22).

[§90] Similarly, for one group, [God] '*bestows on you a double portion of His Mercy*' (57:28); for another, '*God will torment them twice*' (9:101). The reward of one group '*will be doubled for them and for them there will be a rich reward*' (57:18), and for another group '*their*

131. Cf. *Rawḍa* (pp. 151–152§456) on the virgins of Paradise: 'These are a form presented as one feels desire all of a sudden within oneself. The meaning of this is that the subtle realities of the intelligible realm [which] a man has the desire to perceive, take a form presenting itself to his essence, that is, to his rational discriminating soul, and from that he enjoys perceptual happiness and beatitude. [In other words] a marriage is celebrated between the first and last principles of his Gnostic knowledge, the offspring of which are angelic forms and holy spirits.'

punishment will be doubled' (11:20). Such a disparity is due to a discrepancy that exists between good and evil deeds in relation to each class of people, because 'The virtues of the righteous ones are sins for those who are close to God.'[132] There is a great difference between the sin of Adam and that of Iblis. The Prophet says: 'A sword-strike in the Battle of the Ditch (*Khandaq*) is equal to the good deeds of both worlds.'[133]

[§91] Thus, above all rewards, there is the reward of those who, by the decree of Hereafter, discard their very self: 'Above all good deeds there is another, until one dies in the path of God.' Similarly, above all torments there is the torment of those who, for the sake of this world, attend to their very self: '*those who have ruined their souls*' (6:12).

[§92] Those whose deeds are united with reward, they are the people of incalculable bliss (*fawz-i akbar*): '*No human being can imagine what blissful delight, as yet hidden, awaits them*' (32:17). It belongs to them: '[Such a joy] that no eye has ever seen and no ear has ever heard, and it has never been visualized by human thought.'[134] They are above reward and punishment because reward and punishment are both forbidden (*ḥarām*) to the man of God: 'This world is forbidden to the people of the Hereafter, and the Hereafter is forbidden to the people of this world, and both of them are forbidden to the people of God.'[135]

[§93] This is what was possible to write at this time. The expectation is that those who look at these chapters may not withhold their affectionate prayers [for the author], and rectify the correctable mistakes. God is more knowledgeable and a better judge, and He is sufficient and enough for us.

[§94] End of the book, with the assistance of the bounteous Lord, in the evening of the Sunday, al-Nayrūz [*nawrūz*] in the Jalālī calen-

132. Text in Arabic.

133. A Prophetic tradition cited in Bursī, *Mashāriq*, p. 312.

134. A Prophetic tradition cited by M. Aḥmad Qurṭubī in *al-Jāmiʿ li-aḥkām al-Qurʾān* (Cairo, 1967), p. 105; and L. Badakhshī, *Thamarāt al-quds*, p. 1344.

135. A Prophetic tradition. See note 54 above.

dar,[136] the early days of the month of Rabīʿ al-awwal in the year 723 [12 Rabīʿ I/21 March, 1323]. Copied by His servant, who is in need of God's affection, al-Ḥājj Abū Muḥammad, Muḥammad b. Abī al-Fatḥ Masʿūd, May God forgive him.

136. The 21st March corresponds to the first day of the month of Farwardīn, the beginning of the Iranian New Year.

Bibliography

'Abd al-Bāqī, Muḥammad Fu'ād. *al-Mu'jam al-mufahras lis-alfaẓ al-Qur'an al-Karīm*. Beirut, 1945.

Āmidī, Nā'im al-Dīn 'Abd al-Wāḥid b. Muḥammad. *Ghurar al-ḥikam wa durar al-kilam*. Ṣaydā, Lebanon 1931.

Amir-Moezzi, Mohammad Ali. 'Eschatology in Imami Shi'ism', *Encyclopaedia Iranica*, vol. 8 (1998), pp. 575–581.

___ 'Walāya', *in Journal of the American Oriental Society*, 122 (2002), pp. 722–741.

Aristotle. *De Anima*, tr. W. S. Hett. Cambridge, MA, 1936.

Arnaldez, R. 'Ma'ād', in *The Encyclopaedia of Islam*, 2nd ed. (*EI2*).

Badakhshī, Mīrzā La'l Bayk. *Thamarāt al-quds min shajarāt al-uns*, ed. Kamāl Ḥāj-Sayed-Jawādī. Tehran, 1997.

Bukhārī, Muḥammad b. Ismā'īl. *Kitāb al-Jāmi' al-ṣaḥīḥ*, ed. and tr. Muḥammad Asad. Cairo, 1932.

Bursī, Ḥāfiẓ Rajab. *Mashāriq al-anwār al-yaqīn fī ḥaqā'iq asrār amīr al-mu'minīn*, Tehran, n.d.

Corbin, Henry. *Cyclical Time and Ismaili Gnosis*. London, 1983.

Dabashi H. 'The Philosopher/Vizier: Khwāja Naṣīr al-Dīn al-Ṭūsī and the Isma'ilis' in F. Daftary, ed., *Mediaeval Isma'ili History and Thought*. Cambridge, 1996, pp. 231–245.

Daftary, Farhad. 'Ḥasan-i Ṣabbāḥ and the Origins of the Nizārī Isma'ili Movement', in Daftary, ed., *Mediaeval Isma'ili History and Thought*, pp. 181–204, reprinted in his *Ismailis in Medieval Muslim Societies*. London, 2005, pp. 124–148.

___ 'Nasir al-Din al-Tusi and the Ismailis', in his *Ismailis in Medieval Muslim Societies*, pp. 171–182.

___ *The Ismā'īlīs: Their History and Doctrines*. 2nd revised ed., Cambridge, 2007.

Dakake, Maria M. *The Charismatic Community: Shi'ite Identity in Early*

Islam. New York, 2007.

Gardet, L. '*Ḳiyāma*', in *EI2*.

al-Ghazzālī, Abū Ḥāmid. *Kitāb dhikr al-mawt wa-mā baʿduhu*, tr. T. J. Winter as *The Remembrance of Death and Afterlife*. Cambridge, 1989.

Haft bāb-i Bābā Sayyidnā, in W. Ivanow, *Two Early Ismaili Treatises*. Bombay, 1933, pp. 4–44.

Halm, Heinz. 'The Ismaʿili Oath of Allegiance (*ʿahd*) and the 'Sessions of Wisdom' (*majālis al-ḥikma*) in Fatimid Times', in Daftary, *Mediaeval Ismaʿili History and Thought*, pp. 91–115.

Ḥasanzāda Āmulī, Ḥasan. *Āghāz wa anjām-i Khawāja Naṣīr al-Dīn Ṭūsī: Muqaddima wa sharḥ wa taʿlīqāt*. Qumm, 1366 Sh./1987.

Hodgson, M. G. *The Order of Assassins: The Struggle of the Nizārī Ismāʿīlīs against the Islamic World*. The Hague, 1955.

Ibn Māja, Sunan, *Jamʿ jawāmiʿ al-aḥādith wa al-asānīd*. Liechtenstein, 2000.

Ibn Sīnā. *al-Ishārāt wa al-tanbīhāt*, ed. S. Dunyā. Cairo, 1960.

Kāshānī, ʿAbd ʿAhd al-Razzāq.*Taʾwīlāt*, also known as *Tafsīr Ibn ʿArabī*. Beirut, 2001.

al-Kulaynī, Abū Jaʿfar Muḥammad b. Yaʿqūb b. Isḥāq. *al-Uṣūl min al-Kāfī*. Arabic ed. and Persian trans. by Muḥammad Bāqir Kamaraʾī. Tehran, 1956; repr. 1972.

Landolt, Hermann, Samira Sheikh and Kutub Kassam, ed. *An Anthology of Ismaili Literature: A Shiʿi Vision of Islam*. London, 2008.

MacCulloch, J. A. 'Eschatology', in *Encyclopaedia of Religion and Ethics*, ed. James Hastings (Edinburgh, 1994),

Madelung, Wilferd. 'Naṣīr al-Dīn Ṭūsī's Ethics between Philosophy, Shiʿism and Sufism', in R. G. Hovannisian, ed., *Ethics in Islam*. Malibu, CA, 1985.

____ 'Ḳāʾim Āl-i Muḥammad', *EI2*.

____ 'al-Mahdī', *EI2*.

Majlisī, Muḥammad Bāqir. *Biḥār al-anwār: fī aḥādīth ahl al-bayt*. Tehran, 1956–1972.

Massignon, Louis. *Salmān Pāk et les prémices spirituelles de l'Islam Iranien*. Tours, 1934.

al-Miṣrī, Ḥusayn Mujīb. *al-Ṣaḥābī al-jalīl Salmān al-Fārisī ʿind al-ʿArab wa al-Furs wa al-Turk*. Cairo, 1973.

al-Muʾayyad fiʾl-Dīn al-Shīrāzī, *al-Majālis al-Muʾayyadiyya*, vol. 2, ed. Ḥ. Ḥamīd al-Dīn. Oxford, 1986.

Mudarris-i Raḍawī, Muḥammad Taqī. *Yādbūd-i haft ṣadumīn sāl-i Khwāja*

Naṣīr al-Dīn Ṭūsī. Tehran, 1335 Sh./1956.

___*Aḥwāl wa āthār-i Abū Ja'far Muḥammad b. Muḥammad b. Ḥasan al-Ṭūsī*. 2nd ed., Tehran, 1354 Sh./1975.

Mudarrisī Zanjānī, Muḥammad. *Sargudhasht wa 'aqa'id-i falsafī-yi Khwāja Naṣīr al-Dīn Ṭūsī*. Tehran, 1335 Sh./1956.

Nahj al-balāgha, ed. Ṣubḥī al-Ṣāliḥ. Beirut, 1967.

Narāqī, Muḥammad Mahdī. *Jāmi' al-sa'ādāt*, ed. Muḥammad Riḍā Āl-i Muẓaffar. Najaf, 1963.

Nāṣir-i Khusraw. *Dīwān*, ed. Mujtabā Minuwī and Mahdī Muḥaqqiq. Tehran, 1974.

Nasr, Seyyed Hossein. 'Shi'ism and Sufism: Their Relationship in Essence and in History', in his *Sufi Essays*. London, 1970.

Plato. *Phaedro*, tr. R. Hackforth. Cambridge, 1955.

____ *The Republic*, tr. F. M. Cornford. Oxford, 1941.

Pourjavady, Nasrollah. 'Awṣāf al-Ashrāf', in N. Pourjavady and Z. Vesel, ed., *Naṣīr al-Dīn Ṭūsī, Philosophe et savant du XIIIe siècle*. Tehran, 2000. pp. 39–40.

al-Qāḍī al-Nu'mān, Abū Ḥanīfa. *Da'ā'im al-Islām*, ed. Asaf A. A. Fyzee. Cairo, 1951–1961, 2 vols.; English trans. Asaf A. A. Fyzee and revised by Ismail K. Poonawala as *The Pillars of Islam*. New Delhi, 2 vols, 2002–2004.

Qurṭubī, Muḥammad b. Aḥmad. *al-Jāmi' li-aḥkām al-Qur'ān*. Cairo, 1967.

Reyshahrī, Muḥammad. *Mīzān al-ḥikma*. Tehran, 1998.

Ṣadr al-Dīn Shīrāzī. *al-Ḥikma al-muta'āliya fī al-aṣfār al-arba'a*. Tehran, 1977.

Ṣaḥīḥ Muslim. Riyadh, 1999.

Sanā'ī, Majdūd b. Ādam. *Dīwān*, ed. M. Taqī Mudarris-i Raḍawī. Tehran, 1365 Sh./1986, repr. 2006.

Shahrastānī, Abū al-Fatḥ Muḥammad b. 'Abd al-Karīm. *Kitāb al-milal wa al-niḥal*, Persian trans. Jalālī Nā'īnī. Tehran, 1321Sh./1942.

___ *Nihāyat al-aqdām fī 'ilm al-kalām*, ed. and tr. A. Guillaume as *Summa Philosophiae*. London, 1934.

___ *Kitāb al-Muṣāra'a*, ed. and tr. Wilferd Madelung and Toby Mayer as *Struggling with the Philosopher: A Refutation of Avicenna's Metaphysics*. London, 2001.

Smith, Jane Idleman and Yvonne Yazbeck Haddad. *The Islamic Understanding of Death and Resurrection*. New York, 1981.

Sobhani, Ja'far. *Doctrines of Shi'i Islam*, tr. Reza Shah-Kazemi, London, 2001.

Suyūṭī, ʿAbd al-Raḥmān b. Abī Bakr (Jalāl al-Dīn). *al-Jāmiʿ al-ṣaqīr fī aḥādith al-bashīr al-nadhīr*, ed. ʿAbd al-Raʾūf al-Munāwī. Cairo, 1954

Ṭabāṭabaʾī, Muḥammad Ḥusayn. *al-Mīzān fī tafsīr al-Qurʾān*. Tehran, 1974.

Tāmir, ʿĀrif. *Arbaʿa rasāʾil Ismāʿīlīyya*. Salamiyya, Syria, 1952; Beirut, 1953.

Tihrānī, Ḥasan. *Imām-shināsī*. Tehran, 1404/1983–1984.

Tihrānī, Thaqafī. *Rawān-i jāwīd*. Tehran, 1399/1978.

Ṭūsī, Naṣīr al-Dīn Muḥammad b. Muḥammad. *Akhlāq-i Muḥtashimī*, ed. Muḥammad Taqī Dānish-pazhūh. Tehran, 1339 Sh./1960.

___ *Akhlāq-i Nāṣirī*, ed. Mujtabā Mīnuwī and ʿA. R. Ḥaydarī. Tehran, 1356 Sh./1977; tr. G. M. Wickens as *The Nasirean Ethics*. London, 1964.

___ *Asās al-iqtibās*, ed. M. Mudarris-i Raḍawī. Tehran, 1335 Sh./1956.

___ *Awṣāf al-ashrāf*, ed. Māyil Harawī. Mashhad, 1361 Sh./1982.

___ *Majmūʿa-yi rasāʾil*, ed. M. T. Mudarris Raḍawī. Tehran, 1335 Sh./1956.

___ *Maṣāriʿ al-muṣāriʿ*, ed. Ḥasan al-Muʿizzī. Qumm, 1405/1984.

___ *Rawḍa-yi taslīm*, ed. and tr. S. J. Badakhchani as *Paradise of Submission: A Medieval Treatise on Ismaili Thought*. London, 2005.

___ *Risālat al-imāma*, in *Talkhīs al-muḥaṣṣal*, pp. 424–433.

___ *Sayr wa sulūk*, ed. and tr. S. J. Badakhchani as *Contemplation and Action: The Spiritual Autobiography of a Muslim Scholar*. London, 1998.

___ *Sharḥ al-ishārāt wa al-tanbīhāt*. Tehran, 1377/1957.

___ *Tajrīd al-iʿtiqād*, ed. Abū al-Ḥasan Shaʿrānī as *Kashf al-murād*. Tehran, 1974.

___ *al-Tadhkīra fi al-haʾya*, ed. and tr. F. G. Ragep in his *Naṣīr al-Dīn Ṭūsī's Memoir on Astronomy*. New York, 1993, pp. 89– 341.

___ *Talkhīṣ al-muḥaṣṣal*, ed. A. A. Nūrānī, Tehran, 1359 Sh./1980.

Waldman, M. R. 'Islamic Eschatology', under 'Eschatology', in *The Encyclopaedia of Religion*, ed. Lindsay Jones, vol. 4, London, 2005.

Wensinck, A. J., ed. *al-Muʿjam al-mufahras li-alfāḍ al-ḥadīth al-nabawī*. Leiden, 1965.

Werblowsky, R. J. Zwi. 'Eschatology', in the *Encyclopaedia of Religion*, vol. 4, pp. 2833–2840.

Index

سه رساله
از تصنیفات خواجه نصیرالدین
طوسی

متن فارسی و ترجمه انگلیسی
تولا و تبرا، مطلوب المؤمنین و آغاز و انجام

ویرایش و ترجمه
از
سیدجلال حسینی بدخشانی

تولّا و تبرّا

بِسْمِ اللهِ الرَّحْمَنِ الرَّحِيمِ

الحمد لله رب العالمين
و صلواته علی سیدنا محمد و آله الطاهرین[۱]

[§۱] هرکه خواهد دیندار باشد او را از دو چیز چاره نبود: یکی تولا و دیگر تبرا، چنانکه فرموده اند: الدین هو الحب فی الله و البغض [فی الله]. یعنی دین دوستی است در راه خدا و دشمنی در راه خدا. وچون برادر دینی نجیب الدین حسن وفقه الله لما یرضیه، از ین ضعیف محمد طوسی التماس کرد که در این باب شرحی بنویسد و تأکید فرمود، چاره ندید از آنکه کلمه ای چند از سخن پیشوایان دین و معلمان اهل یقین – خصوصاً معلم وقت پادشاه بزرگوار ناصر الدنیا والدین شهریار ایران عبد الرحیم بن ابی منصور، اعلی الله امره و حرس ظله المبارک – جهت آن برادر دینی ثبت کرد.

[§۲] اکنون گوئیم مردم را دو قوت است که آن دو قوت در وی از فروع و شاخهای نفس بهیمی است و آن شهوت و غضب است. یعنی آرزو و خشم که در دیگر جانوران نیز این دو قوت موجود است و بایست و نبایست عبارت از این دو قوت است. ولکن مردم را نفسی

دیگر است که دیگر جانوران را نیست و آن را نفس ناطقه خوانند، یعنی نفس گویا و عقلی است که آنرا به پارسی خرد خوانند.

[§۳] و می باید که نفس بهیمی که آرزو و خشم از قوت های آن است در فرمان نفس گویای انسانی باشد ونفس گویا در فرمان عقل و عقل در فرمان فرمانده حقیقت که او را معلم دین خوانند تا حرکت او بر استقامت بود. و اگر به خلاف این باشد، حرکت منکوس و نگونسار بود. یعنی خرد در فرمان نفس گویا بود و نفس گویا در فرمان نفس بهیمی تا بر پی آرزو و خشم شود و به هاویه یعنی به دوزخ بود. نعوذ بالله منه.

[§۴] پس هرگاه نفس بهیمی در فرمان نفس گویا آید آن شهوت و غضب از آنچه بوده اند لطیف تر شوند. شهوت از شهوتی فراتر آید و به درجه شوقی برسد وغضب از غضبی فراتر آید و به درجه اعراض رسد. پس در آنکس که نفس گویای او بر نفس بهیمی غالب شود، بجای شهوت و غضب شوق و اعراض بود. وچون نفس گویا در فرمان عقل باشد آن شوق و اعراض لطیف تر و کامل تر شود [و] به ارادت و کراهت بدل شود. و همچنین چون عقل در فرمان فرمانده حقیقت آید آن ارادت و کراهت به تولا و تبرا بدل شود.

[§۵] و حقیقت تولا روی فرا کسی کردن است و حقیقت [تبرا از جز او بیزار شد]ن. و او آنگاه باشد که آرزو و خشم او به دوستی مؤدی و روی فرا او کردن، و د[شمنی و از هرچه جز اوست بیزار شدن، مبدل شو]د. و اگر نه چنین باشد چون نفس گویا تبع نفس بهیمی شود، با آرزو و خشم دو [چیز دیگر اضافت شو]د هم از آن باب یکی حب مال و دیگر حب جاه. و چون خرد تبع نفس گویا شود دو چیز دیگر با آن اضافت شود یکی حرص و دیگر کِبر. ودیگر اخلاق بد ازین اخلاق برخیزد تا مردم را به جائی رساند که هیچ خُلق بد در وجود نباشد إلا که در او موجود باشد. آنگاه به هلاکت ابدی انجامد. نعوذ با لله منه.

[§۶] اما آن کس که حرکت او مستقیم بود، اگر نفس بهیمی او [را] فرا شهوت دارد، نفس گویا چون براو غالب بود، آن شهوت را با عفت بدل کند. عفت یعنی پاک نفسی. وچون او را فرا غضب دارد، نفس گویا آن غضب را با حلم بدل کند. [حلم] یعنی مداراه و سکون. وچون نفس گویا او را فرا حُب مال دارد، عقل آنرا به ایثار بدل کند. یعنی دیگران را بر خود برگزیدن. وچون نفس گویا او را فرا حب جاه دارد، عقل آنرا با عُزلت و انقطاع یعنی از خلق بُبریدن بدل کند. وچون او را فرا حرص دارد آمر امر آن حرص را با قناعت بدل کند. وچون او را فرا کِبر دارد آمر آنرا با تواضع بدل کند. و این اخلاق ستوده اصول دیگر اخلاق

شوند تا هر خُلق نیکو که در مردم ممکن بود در او حاصل شود و آنگاه به سعادت ابدی رسد، إن شاء مولانا.

[§۷] و تولا و تبرا را ظاهری است و باطنی: تولا را ظاهر آن است که روی فرا نیکان کنند و تبرا را ظاهر آنکه از بدان بیزار شوند. وتولا را باطن آنکه روی فرا مرد خدا کنند، یعنی محق[۲] یگانه که اصل همه نیکی ها اوست. و تبرا را باطن آنکه از هرچه جز اوست بیزار شوند.

[§۸] تولا به دو چیز ممکن شود: به معرفت و محبت. چه تا مردم خدا را نشناسند و او را دوست ندارند روی فرا او نکنند. و معرفت شناختن است و محبت دوستی. و تبرا [نیز] به دو چیز ممکن شود: هجرت و جهاد. هجرت از غیر او بُبریدن است و جهاد کوشش کردن. چه تا از غیر او نبرند و با دشمنان او کوشش نکنند تبرا تمام نشود.

[§۹] و این چهار چیز که تولا و تبرا بی آن تمام نیست، یعنی معرفت و محبت و هجرت و جهاد، هر یکی را ظاهری و باطنی باشد: ظاهر معرفت آن است که خدا را بشناسند و باطنش انکه جز او را نشناسند و ظاهر محبت آنکه او را دوست دارند و باطنش آنکه جز او را دوست ندارند. و ظاهر جهاد آنکه با دشمنان او کوشش کنند و[باطن آن آنکه]

مال و جاه و زن و فرزند در راه او بذل کنند و [ظاهر هجرت آنکه] شهوت و غضب [در راه او بذل کنند و باطن آن آنکه] حب جاه و بایست و نبایست در راه او نیست گردانند. و چون این جمله کرده باشند شرط تولا و تبرا بجای آورده باشند و بعد از آن کمال دین داری در رضا و تسلیم باشد.

[§۱۰] و رضا و تسلیم بعد از ان حاصل آید که تولا و تبرا یکی شده باشد و آن چنان بود که تبرا در تولا مستغرق گردانند، هم چنانکه اضافت در حقیقت و مستأنف در مفروغ و شریعت در قیامت تا تولای صِرف حاصل شود که آن تولا و تبرا که در اول داشت در این تولا [و تبرا] ی آخر حاصل باشد. و این آن گاه میسر شود که بایست و نبایست هردو یکی شوند. نبایست در بایست مستغرق گردد و محبت و معرفت هردو یکی شود. محبت در معرفت مستغرق گردد. مرد [اگر] جز او را نبیند از که تبرا کند. [و اگر] جز او را نشناسد، نخواست او چه چیز را؟

[§۱۱] و چون چنین باشد همه حالات دنیا او را یکسان شود. به هرچه آید راضی باشد. به هیچ شادی خوش نه گردد [و] از هیچ اندوه دل تنگ نشود. بر هیچ گذشته حسرت نخورد [و] به هیچ آینده امید ندارد.

و چون چنین باشد درجه رضا که آن درجه خوشنودی باشد بیافته باشد. یعنی به آنچه آید خرسند و راضی باشد و از خدای تعالی خوشنود، و آن گاه از خدای تعالی نیز امیدوار باشد که از او خوشنود شود.

[§۱۲] و نشان رضا سه چیز بود: یکی آن که بدانچه بدو رسد از خیر بشاشت نه نماید و آنچه بدو رسد از شرّ بدان دلتنگ نشود. و دیگر آنکه هرچه او را فرا دارند فرا ایستد و اعتراض نه کند و دلتنگ نشود. اگر به خیرش فرا دارند یا به شر. چون دانند که فرمان فرمانده حقیقی است در خویشتن تفاوتی نیارد و به یک طرف میل زیادت از آن نه کند که به طرف دیگر. مثلاً اگر گویند راحتی به کسی رسان یا گویند رنجی به کسی رسان، در خود تفاوتی نیابد. و سیم آنکه بر هیچ آفریده ای از خود اعتراض نیارد و نفرت نه کند و نه گوید فلان نیک است و فلان بد و فلان خیّر و فلان شریر. بل اگر چیزی فرا زفان او دهند یا فرا دل او، چون از قبل معلم دین باشد، فرا گیرد و به خودی[۳] خود در هیچ کار نه ایستد. پس هرگاه که این نشان ها در خود بیافت به درجه رضا رسیده باشد.

[§۱۳] بماند تسلیم. و تسلیم باز سپردن باشد. و باز سپردن آن است که هرآنچه داند که با او به آن جهان نخواهد آمد هم دراین جهان باز سپارد، یعنی دل در آن نبندد و آن در دست خود عاریتی و مجازی شمرد مثلاً چشم و گوش و زبان و دست و پای، بلکه تن و آرزو و هوی و خشم و بایست و نبایست و همچنین قوت های اندرونی چون وهم و دانش و بینش – این همه و آنچه توابع این باشد چون مال و جاه و حرمت و حشمت و غیر آن تا به جان و زندگی جمله عاریتی شمرد چنانکه کسی با امانتی از آن غیری درمانده باشد و در آرزوی آن بود که آن امانت از او باز گیرند و به آن خوشدل باشد و چنان داند که باری از دل او برخاست و از زیر اندوهی عظیم بیرون آمد و از عهده تکلیفی فارغ شد. پس هرگاه که به این درجه رسید که این جمله به نزدیک او ناچیز باشد و دل درآن نبندد به درجه تسلیم رسیده باشد.

[§۱۴] وچون تولا و تبرا و رضا و تسلیم حاصل آمد ایمان حاصل آمده باشد. و إلا اسم مؤمن براو واقع نشود، چنانکه فرموده است: **فَلاَ وَرَبِّكَ لاَ يُؤْمِنُونَ حَتَّىَ يُحَكِّمُوكَ فِيمَا شَجَرَ بَيْنَهُمْ ثُمَّ لاَ يَجِدُواْ فِي أَنفُسِهِمْ حَرَجًا مِّمَّا قَضَيْتَ وَيُسَلِّمُواْ تَسْلِيمًا** (۴:۶۵). یعنی بحق خداوند تو که این مردم ایمان دار نه باشند تا ترا برخود بحاکم نه کنند در هر اختلاف که ایشان را می افتد؛ یعنی در هر حال گردنده که فرا پیش ایشان می آید، پس چنان

شوند که از هر حکم و قضا که تو بر ایشان کنی در دل خود اندوهی و دلتنگی نیابند و باز سپارند آنچه باز سپردنی است باز سپردنی تمام.

[§۱۵] اکنون اینجا مؤمن را سه شرط نهاده است: یکی تحکیم یعنی او را بر خود بحاکم کردن و آن تولا است که تولا و تبرا هر دو در او جمع باشند. و دوم و سیم رضا و تسلیم و چون حال به این درجه رسد مرد مؤمن باشد و بعد از آن باید که موقن شود چه نسبت مؤمن با دنیا چون نسبت موقن باشد با آخرت، چنانکه میفرماید: **يُؤْمِنُونَ بِالْغَيْبِ وَبِالآخِرَةِ هُمْ يُوقِنُونَ** (۲:۳،۴) یعنی ایمان آورده اند به آنچه از ایشان غایب است و به آخرت موقن باشند.

[§۱۶] و ایمان باور داشتن است و ایقان به یقین شدن. باورداشتن گاه بود که با ظن بود و یقین با ظن نبود. وظن حال دنیا است و یقین حال آخرت، چنانکه در کلام مقدس به چند جای بیان فرموده است. و یقین آن است که آخرت را چنان شناخته باشد که گوئی به معاینه همی بیند. و این آن گاه بود که نیستی دنیا و حالات دنیا معاینه بدیده باشد.

[§۱۷] پس هر که دنیا را هست بیند نظر او معکوس بود، لا مُحاله آخرت را نیست بیند. وچون آخرت را هست بیند دنیا را نیست بیند و

این [دو] لازم یکدیگرند. پس مرد یقین آن کس بود که دنیا و حالات دنیا را نیست بیند و چندانکه نظر او از دنیا و حالات دنیا بریده تر باشد بر حال آخرت یقینش زیادت باشد.

[§۱۸] و یقین را سه مرتبه است: یکی را حق الیقین خوانند، یعنی درستی یقین. و دیگر را علم الیقین، یعنی دانستن یقین و سیم را عین الیقین یعنی ذات یقین و حقیقت یقین. وحق الیقین درجه مؤمنانی باشد که از دنیا روی فرا آخرت کرده باشند. وعلم الیقین درجه مؤمنانی باشد که به کمال آخرت رسیده باشند و عین الیقین درجه کسانی باشد که از آخرت بگذرند. و آنها که از آخرت بگذرند اهل وحدت باشند. چه فرموده اند که دنیا بر اهل آخرت حرام است و آخرت بر اهل دنیا حرام است و دنیا و آخرت بر اهل خدا حرام است.

[§۱۹] و مرد به درجه وحدت بعد از آن تواند رسیدن که هستی و نیستی بخود دربازد و نظرش از این دو مرتبه بگذرد. و تا مادام که میان هستی و نیستی متردد بود یا مرد دنیا بود یا مرد آخرت. اگر هستی مجازی و نیستی حقیقی خواهد مرد دنیا است و آخرت بر او حرام است، واگر هستی حقیقی و نیستی مجازی خواهد مرد آخرت است و دنیا بر او حرام است، و اگر نه هستی خواهد و نه نیستی خود —

بلکه نه خود خواهد و نه بیخودی خود و نه این هر دو داند و نه این هر دو بیند — مرد خدا باشد و دنیا و آخرت هر دو بروی حرام باشد.

[§۲۰] یعنی اگر به دنیا یا به آخرت نظر کند از کمال آن درجه بیفتد و معکوس شود. چه مادام که مرد را آخرت و بهشت و ثواب و سعادت باید کمال خود خواسته باشد. وکمال خود بسوی خود خواسته باشد، پس خود را خواسته باشد نه خدا را. و چون چنین بود مرد کثرت بود نه مرد وحدت چنانکه فرماید:

هرچه بینی جز خدا آن بت بود درهم شکن

[§۲۱] پس جز خدا خواستن بت پرستی بود. و آخرت و بهشت و رضا و جوار خدا جز خدا است و ازاین وجه نشاید که طالب وحدت را به هیچ از این التفاتی و میلی باشد، یا خود [را] ازاین جمله شناسد و داند و بیند. چه هرکه خدا را شناسد نشانش آن بود که جز خدا نخواهد و این خدا را شناختن و خدا را خواستن هنوز از کثرت است، چه در وحدت شناسنده و شناخته نباشد، خواست و خواسته نباشد، همه خدا باشد و بس.

[§۲۲] پس آن کس [که] همه خدا بیند و بس طالب وحدت باشد. اگر خدای تعالی حجاب هستی و نیستی از پیش بر گیرد باین مرتبه برسد.

واین مرتبه آن است که در عبارت هیچ آفریده ای نیاید. و هرچه در عبارت آرند از کفر و شرک خالی نبود. پس مرد مجتهد را جهد باید کرد در آنچه جز خدا است از پیش خود بر گیرد تا به خودی خود به خودی خود برسد، إن شاء الله تعالی.

[§۲۳] علق لنفسه.

مطلوب المؤمنين

مطلوب المؤمنين

بِسْمِ اللّهِ الرَّحْمَنِ الرَّحِيمِ

الحمدُ لله الذّی عَرَّفنا بِنفسِهِ، عَلَّمَنا مِن شُکره

وَفَتَحَ لَنا باباً مِن ابواب العِلمِ بِربوبیّته وَدلّنا للإخلاص فِی تُوحیدِه

[§۱] هرچند[۱] کمترین بندگان دعوت هادیه محمد طوسی خود را محل[۲] آن نمی یابد[۳] که از علم سخن گوید اما [چون از] [۴]حضرت علیا لا زال[۵] نافذاً اشارت فرموده اند که [این] بنده آنچه از فصول مبارک و از کتب پیشوایان[۶] دین خوانده و از معلمان[۷] شنیده شمهء با مؤمنان طالب تقریرکند، بنا بر موجب[۸] [از فصول مبارک و کتب پیشوایان دین] انتخابی کرده تا کسانی که طالب راه حق[۹] باشند ایشان را فهم این معانی دشوار نبود.

[§۲] چون ترکیب وجود آدمی از چهار طبایع خالی نیست این مختصر را برابر طبایع چهارگانه بر چهار فصل اختصار کرده شد.[۱۰] واین رساله را مطلوب المؤمنین نام نهاده شد. توقع به کرم عمیم مخادیم[۱۱] و عزیزان و اصحاب [و اخوان] زادهم الله توفیقهم للخیرات [آن است] که چون این مختصر به نظر مبارک ایشان مشرف گردد[۱۲] و لفظ رکیک و یا معنی ناجایگاه و یا سهوی و خطائی بینند آنرا [نتیجه طبع] این بندهء عام ناتمام

دانند و اصلاح در آن ارزانی فرمایند[۱۳] و آنرا از راه مکرمت به ذیل شفقت بپوشانند. و اگر[سخنی ویا] معنی به جایگاه بینند آنرا از جود[۱۴] مبارک خداوند زمان[۱۵] دانند و به سمع رضا استماع فرمایند و این ضعیف ذلیل را به دعای خیر یاد دارند.[۱۶]

فهرست کتاب:[۱۷] **فصل اول** در بیان مبدأ و معاد. **فصل دویم** در بیان مؤمن اسماعیلی. **فصل سیوم** در بیان تولا و تبرا. **فصل چهارم** در بیان هفت ارکان شریعت و تأویل آن.

فصل اول
در بیان مبدأ و معاد

[§۳] مردم[۱۸] عاقل را بباید دانست که مبدأ وجود آدمی از امر[۱۹] باری تعالی به میانجی عقل و نفس و افلاک و انجم و تأثیرات طبایع موجود میشود. واین عالم سفلی اثری است از عالم علوی چنانکه از حکمت الهی و آثار دلائل عقلی معلوم میشود که آفریدگار را سبحانه و تعالی مقصود از آفرینش عالم آدمی[۲۰] است، بدین معنی که لولاک لما خلقت الافلاک.[۲۱] وعلم و معرفتی که در آدمی موجود است در افلاک و انجم و معادن و باقی حیوانات موجود نیست و آدمی را از جمله موجودات برگزیده است بدین معنی: **وَلَقَدْ كَرَّمْنَا بَنِي آدَمَ وَحَمَلْنَاهُمْ فِي الْبَرِّ وَالْبَحْرِ** (۱۷:۷۰).

[§۴] و چون مبدأ وجود آدمی از امر واجب الوجود موجود شد[۲۲] و او شریف تر جوهری است، پس بر آدمی[۲۳] واجب باشد که مبدأ و معاد خود را چنانچه شرط است[۲۴] بداند، یعنی[۲۵] از کجا آمده و بچه کار آمده و بازگشت او به کجا خواهد بود تا خود را و آفرینش عالم را[۲۶] باطل نکرده باشد.

[§۵] واین معنی جز به معرفت آفریدگار حق سبحانه و تعالی حاصل نیست و معرفت آفریدگار جز[۲۷] از رسول علیه السلام و فرزند بحقیقت[۲۸] او که امام زمان و خلیفه [خدا] و وصی و قائم مقام او است حاصل نیست بدین معنی که [**إِنِّي جَاعِلٌ فِي الْأَرْضِ خَلِيفَةً** (۲:۳۰)] و خبر رسول علیه السلام که "لوخلت الأرض من امام ساعة لمادت باهلها."[۲۹]

[§۶] چون کردگار خودرا بدانست و معرفت رسول و امام زمان حاصل کرد مبدأ و معاد خود دانسته باشد و بعد از آن بر وی واجب باشد شرایط بندگی و فرمانبرداری [بجای آوردن] بدین معنی که قوله تعالی: **وَمَا خَلَقْتُ الْجِنَّ وَالْإِنسَ إِلَّا لِيَعْبُدُونِ** (۵۱:۵۶).[۳۰]

[§۷] پس پرستیدن موقوف است به شناخت و شناخت حق تعالی به عقل تنها میسر نمیشود زیرا که معرفت و هر صنعتی که انسان را است بی تعلیم حاصل نمیشود. پس شناختن حق تعالی مشکل ترین چیزها است و حق اولاً آن بود که به تعلیم احتیاج داشته باشد [واین تعلیم به معلمی رسد که او را با کتاب معرفت هیچ احتیاج نباشد.][۳۱]

[§۸] پس بر جوهری [که مقصود آفرینش این عالم او بوده واجب نکند که به مانند حیوان بخورد][۳۲] و بخسبد و به لذات نفسانی مشغول شود [و در اوامر و نواهی تقصیر کند][۳۳] تا از حیوان پستر بود بدین معنی که قوله تعالی: **إِلَّا كَالْأَنْعَامِ بَلْ هُمْ أَضَلُّ سَبِيلًا** (۲۵:۴۴).[۳۴]

[§۹] پس هر وقت که مرد عاقل بر موجب[۳۵] فرمان امام زمان مأمور امر معلم صادق باشد مال و عیال و جان و تن که همه عاریت اند[۳۶] در راه حق بذل کند و وجود خود را به کلی از پیش بردارد[۳۷] و از این عالم مجازی به عالم [لایزالی وجود] حقیقی باز گردد، بدین معنی که[۳۸] کل شیء یرجع إلی اصله با معاد خود رسیده باشد. این است شرط مبدأ و معاد[که یاد کرده شد].[۳۹]

فصل دویم
در بیان مؤمن اسماعیلی

[§۱۰] جماعتی که طالبان دین حق اند و خود را اسماعیلی میدانند باید که شرط مؤمنی و [معنی] اسماعیلی را بدانند. معنی اسماعیلی آن است که هرکه دعوی[۴۰] می کند او را باید سه نشان باشد: اول [آنکه] معرفت امام زمان او را حاصل باشد[۴۱] و مأمور امر[۴۲] معلم صادق باشد و یک لحظه از ذکر و فکر حق تعالی خالی نباشد. دویم رضا، یعنی هرچه بدو رسد از خیر و شر و نفع و ضرر، بدان متغیر نشود و سیّم تسلیم یعنی باز سپردن، و باز سپردن آن باشد که هرچه هست و[با او] به آن جهان نخواهد رفت همه را عاریتی داند وباز سپارد[۴۳] و مال و عیال[۴۴] وباقی حالات دنیائی را در راه حق بذل کند تا به درجه مؤمنی رسیده باشد [بدین معنی که **فَلاَ وَرَبِّكَ لاَ يُؤْمِنُونَ حَتَّىَ يُحَكِّمُوكَ فِيمَا شَجَرَ بَيْنَهُمْ ثُمَّ لاَ يَجِدُواْ فِي أَنفُسِهِمْ حَرَجًا مِّمَّا قَضَيْتَ وَيُسَلِّمُواْ تَسْلِيمًا** (۶۵:۴).][۴۵]

[§۱۱] بعد از آن موقن باید شدن بدین معنی که[۴۶] **يُؤْمِنُونَ بِالْغَيْبِ** (۲:۳) **وَبِالآخِرَةِ هُمْ يُوقِنُونَ** (۴:۲). و موقن را نیز سه نشان باشد: اول حق الیقین، یعنی درستی یقین؛ دویم علم الیقین، یعنی دانستن[۴۷] یقین؛

سیوم عین الیقین، یعنی ذات و حقیقت یقین.[۴۸] حق الیقین درجه مؤمنانی باشد که از دنیا روی به آخرت دارند و علم الیقین درجهء مؤمنانی باشد که به درجهء کمال آخرت رسیده باشند و عین الیقین درجهء مؤمنانی باشد که از [دنیا و][۴۹] آخرت بگذرند و ایشان اهل وحدت باشند.

[§۱۲] و به درجهء وحدت وقتی توان رسید که از هستی خود بکل الوجوه ببرند و بهشت و ثواب و کمال خود نه طلبند[۵۰] و از دنیا و آخرت[۵۱] بگذرند[۵۲] بدین معنی که قال النبی علیه السلام: الدنیا حرام علی اهل الآخرة، والآخرة حرام علی اهل الدنیا و هما حرامان علی اهل الله تعالی. این است شرط مؤمن اسماعیلی که یاد کرده شد.[۵۳]

فصل سوم
در بیان تولا و تبرا

[§۱۳] هرکه دعوی دین داری کند او را از دو چیز چاره نیست: اول تولا و دوم تبرا بدین معنی که الدین هو الحب فی الله و البغض فی الله، و

حقیقت تولا روی با کسی کردن است و حقیقت تبرا از غیر او بیزار شدن.

[§۱۴] و تولا و تبرا را[۵۴] ظاهری و باطنی است. تولای ظاهر آنست که روی با نیکان کنند و تولای باطن آنکه روی به مرد[۵۵] خدا کنند، یعنی امام زمان. تبرای ظاهر آنکه از بدان ببرند و بیزار شوند و تبرای باطن آنکه از هرچه جز خدا است[۵۶] بیزار شوند.

[§۱۵] و تولا و تبرا به چهار چیز تمام شود: اول معرفت، دویم محبت، سیوم هجرت وچهارم جهاد. و[۵۷] هریک را ظاهر و باطنی است. ظاهر معرفت آنکه خدای را به [مرد خدا] [۵۸] یعنی امام زمان که خلیفه اوست شناسند و باطنش آنکه غیر اورا نشناسند. ظاهر محبت آنکه او را[۵۹] و دوست دارند و باطنش آنکه غیر او را دوست ندارند. [ظاهر هجرت آنکه از دشمنان او ببرند و بیزار باشند و باطنش آنکه هرچه] [۶۰] جز اوست چون مال و عیال و جان و تن[۶۱] از همه ببرند.[۶۲] ظاهر جهاد آنکه با دشمنان حق دشمنی کنند و باطنش آنکه با خود در ترک لذات و شهوات کوشش نمایند[۶۳] و همه را در راه حق نیست گردانند. چون این معانی را بجای آورده باشند تولا و تبرای حقیقی درست شده باشد. این است شرط تولا و تبرا.[۶۴]

فصل چهارم
در بیان هفت ارکان شریعت و تأویل آن

[§۱۶] به نزدیک همه طائفه روشن است که پیشتر از ظاهر به باطن هیچ چیز نتوانند رسید. و هر چیزی که موجود است او را ظاهری و باطنی هست. [مثلاً ظاهرکه عالم سفلی است و باطن که عالم علوی است و هرچه دراین عالم سفلی که ظاهر است موجود است و در عالم باطن موجود خواهد شد].[۶۵]

[§۱۷] اول ظاهر شریعت آنکه پوست موجود میشود بعد از آن مغز و دانه و بار که مقصود است به کمال میرسد. پس هرکه دعوی خداپرستی کند باید اول ظاهر شریعت که مثل پوست است به ظاهر[۶۶] کار بندد و اوامر و نواهی[۶۷] هفت ارکان شریعت بر قانون شریعت بجای آوردو بعد از آنکه ارکان ظاهری را بجای آورده باشد و خواهد که معنی باطن[۶۸] را بداند و به دانش از این عالم بدان عالم باطن باز گردد و به مقام اصلی خود باز رسد براین موجب باید که هفت ارکان حقیقت را بجای آورد تا مرد حقیقت باشد.

[§۱۸] اول شهادت و شهادت آن باشد که خدای را به امام زمان شناسند بدین معنی که **إِنِّي جَاعِلٌ فِي الأَرْضِ خَلِيفَةً** (۲:۳۰). دوم طهارت و طهارت آن باشد که از آئین و سنت گذشته دست بداری و هرچه امام زمان فرماید حق[۶۹] دانی و مطیع امر او باشی. بدین معنی که قوله تعالی: یَا **أَيُّهَا الَّذِينَ آمَنُواْ أَطِيعُواْ اللهَ وَأَطِيعُواْ الرَّسُولَ وَأُوْلِي الأَمْرِ مِنكُمْ** (۴:۵۹). سیّم نماز است و نماز آن است که یک نفس از طاعت خدا[۷۰] و خلیفه خدا غافل نباشند تا پیوسته در نماز باشند بدین معنی که **الَّذِينَ هُمْ عَلَى صَلَاتِهِمْ دَائِمُونَ** (۲۳:۷۰). چهارم روزه است و روزه آن باشد که هفت [اندام] اعضای خود را از ظاهر وباطن به فرمان خدای بسته داری بدین معنی که قوله تعالی: **إِنِّي نَذَرْتُ لِلرَّحْمَنِ صَوْمًا** (۱۹:۲۶).[۷۱] پنجم زکوة و زکوة آن باشد که هرچه خدای تعالی به تو ارزانی داشته باشد[۷۲] به برادر مؤمن ارزانی داری و حق فقرا و مساکین باز مگیرید بدین معنی که قوله تعالی: **وَيُؤْتُوا الزَّكَاةَ وَذَلِكَ دِينُ الْقَيِّمَةِ** (۹۸:۵) ششم جهاد است و جهاد آن است که با نفس و هوای خود جنگ کنی[۷۳] و از هرچه جز خدای باشد ببُری و جان و تن خود را در راه حق بذل کنی بدین معنی: **وَجَاهَدُواْ فِي سَبِيلِ اللهِ بِأَمْوَالِهِمْ وَأَنفُسِهِمْ** (۹:۲۰). هفتم حج است و حج آن باشد که دست از این سرای فانی بداری و طلب سرای بقا[۷۴] کنی بدین معنی که **وَمَا هَذِهِ الْحَيَاةُ الدُّنْيَا إِلَّا**

لَهْوٌ وَلَعِبٌ وَإِنَّ الدَّارَ الْآخِرَةَ لَهِيَ الْحَيَوَانُ لَوْ كَانُوا يَعْلَمُونَ (۲۹:۶۴). و این است طریقهء اهل باطن.

[§۱۹] و باید که تأویل هفت ارکان شریعت برین موجب که یاد کرده شد بجای آورد تا مرد حقیقت باشند و یقین بدانند که اوامر و نواهی و تکالیف شرعی بسیار آسان تر است از تکالیف حقیقی بدان سبب که مرد شریعت هر طاعتی که بر وی بحکم شریعت واجب باشد به دو ساعت در شبانه روزی توانند کرد[۷۵] و بعد ازآن به هر مهم و کسب وکار دنیوی که باشد مشغول شوند و به حکم شریعت خدا پرست و رستگار بود. و اوامر و نواهی حقیقت دشوار تر است بدان سبب که مرد حقیقت اگر طرفة العینی از نماز و روزه و طاعت[۷۶] باز ماند و غافل شود در آن وقت هرچه کند و بیند نه به سوی خدا باشد، بلکه اگرشربت آبی یا لقمه خورد و نیت او آن باشد که گرسنگی و تشنگی به آن آب و لقمه رفع شود آن آب و لقمه بر او حرام باشد بحکم حقیقت و او مرد حقیقت و اهل باطن نبود بلکه هر طاعتی که کرده باشد ضایع بود و او خدا پرست و رستگار نبود. جماعتی که خود را بدین قوت نمی بینند و به اوامر و نواهی حقیقی قیام نمی توانند نمود اولی آن که دست از طاعت شریعت کوتاه نکند که خسر الدنیا و الآخره باشد. و هرکه خلاف

این معنی کند نه مرد شریعت بود و نه مرد حقیقت، بی شک ملحد و بی دین باشد.

[§۲۰] و حق تعالی همگنان را توفیق طاعت ظاهر و باطن ارزانی داراد و بر امر حق تعالی و فرمان امام زمان و متابعت قرآن و اخبار رسول علیه السلام ثابت قدم داراد و از وسوس شیطانی و جور و ظلم ظالمان و بلای ناگهان و فتنه های آخر زمان در امان خود بدارد وگوشه عافیتی وکفاف معیشتی ارزانی داراد.[۷۷]

آغاز و انجام

یا

« تذکره »

بِسْمِ اللهِ الرَّحْمَنِ الرَّحِيمِ[۱]

رَبَّنَا لاَ تُزِغْ قُلُوبَنَا بَعْدَ إِذْ هَدَيْتَنَا وَهَبْ لَنَا مِن لَّدُنكَ رَحْمَةً إِنَّكَ أَنتَ الْوَهَّابُ

رَبَّنَا إِنَّكَ جَامِعُ النَّاسِ لِيَوْمٍ لاَّ رَيْبَ فِيهِ

إِنَّ اللّهَ لاَ يُخْلِفُ الْمِيعَادَ (۸:۳-۹).

[§۱] سپاس آفریدگاری را که آغاز همه اوست و انجام همه باوست، بلکه خود همه اوست. و درُود[۲] بر برگزیدگان[۳] که راهنمایان خلقند بآغاز و انجام خصوصا بر محمد[۴] و آلش علیهم السلام.[۵]

[§۲] اما بعد، دوستی عزیز[۶] از مُحرر این **تذکره** <محمد بن محمد الطوسی>[۷] التماس کرد که نبذی چند[۸] از آنچه سالکان راه آخرت مشاهده کرده اند[۹] از <انجام کار آفرینش>[۱۰] شبیه به آنچه در کتاب الهی[۱۱] مسطور است و بر زبان انبیاء و اولیاء[۱۲] مذکور، علیهم السلام، از احوال قیامت[۱۳] و بهشت و دوزخ و غیر آن ثبت کند[۱۴] برآن وجه که اهل بینش به عیان می بینند،[۱۵] <نه بدان گونه که اهل دانش بیان میکنند.>[۱۶] هرچند اجابت[۱۷] این التماس مُتعذّر بود بحکم آنکه نه هرچه هست نصیب هر کس[۱۸] است، و نه هر چه نصیب کس است بتواند

دیدن، و نه هرچه بیند بتواند دانست، و نه هرچه بداند بتواند گفت، و نه هرچه بگوید بتواند نوشت.[۱۹] چه اگر دیدن بعین بود، دانستن باثر تواند بود، <و اگر دانستن به تصور بود، گفتن به اخبار تواند بود، و اگر گفتن به تصریح نوشتن به تعریض و تلویح تواند بود:>[۲۰] لیس الخبر کالمعاینه، فکیف اذا کان الخبر بالایماءِ والإشارة. اما چون خاطرش بآن مُتلطِّف[۲۱] بود چاره ندیدم[۲۲] از اسعاف[۲۳] بآنچه ممکن شد.[۲۴] پس اگر این تذکره از آنچه مراد آن عزیز است قاصر باشد باید که چون عذر واضح است مواخذت نفرماید،[۲۵] < و او و دیگر متأملان به عین رضا ملاحظه و مطالعه کنند و خللی که ببینند اصلاح واجب شمرند.>[۲۶] **وَمَا تَوْفِيقِي إِلاَّ بِاللهِ عَلَيْهِ تَوَكَّلْتُ وَإِلَيْهِ أُنِيبُ** (۱۱:۸۸). **إِنَّ هَذِهِ تَذْكِرَةٌ فَمَن شَاء اتَّخَذَ إِلَى رَبِّهِ سَبِيلًا. وَمَا تَشَاؤُونَ إِلَّا أَن يَشَاء اللَّهُ إِنَّ اللَّهَ كَانَ عَلِيمًا حَكِيمًا. يُدْخِلُ مَن يَشَاء فِي رَحْمَتِهِ وَالظَّالِمِينَ أَعَدَّ لَهُمْ عَذَابًا أَلِيمًا**(۷۶:۲۹-۳۱). اللهم ارنا الحق حقا وارزقنا اتباعه، وأرنا الباطل باطلا وارزقنا اجتنابه وادخلنا فی رحمتک بحق المصطفی من عبادک[۲۷] إنک علی کل شی قدیر <وانت حسبنا>[۲۸]

[§۳] < **ابتداء شروع در مطلب**>[۲۹] وضع اساس این تذکره بر بیست فصل اتفاق افتاد و فهرست فصول این است:[۳۰]

فصل اول: در صفت راه آخرت و ذکر سالکانش واسباب اعراض مردم از آن و ذکر آفات آن اعراض.

فصل دوم: در اشارت به مبدأ ومعاد وآمدن از فطرت اولی و رسیدن به آنجا و ذکر شب قدر و روز قیامت.

فصل سیم: در اشارت به هر دو جهان و ذکر مراتب مردم در این جهان و در آن جهان.

فصل چهارم: در اشارت به زمان و مکان اخرت.

فصل پنجم: در اشارت به حشر خلایق.

فصل ششم: در اشارت به احوال اصناف خلق در آن جهان و ذکر بهشت و دوزخ.

فصل هفتم: در اشارت به صراط.

فصل هشتم: در اشارت به صحایف اعمال و کرام الکاتبین و نزول ملائکه و شیاطین به نیکان و بدان.

فصل نهم: در اشارت به حساب و به طبقات اهل حساب.

فصل دهم: در اشارت به وزن اعمال و ذکر میزان.

فصل یازدهم: در اشارت به طیّ آسمان ها.

فصل دوازدهم: در اشارت به نفخات صور و تبدیل زمین وآسمان.

فصل سیزدهم: در اشارت به حال هائی که در روز قیامت حادث شود و وقوف خلق به عرصات.

فصل چهاردهم: در اشارت به درهای بهشت و دوزخ.

فصل پانزدهم: در اشارت به زبانیهء دوزخ.

فصل شانزدهم: در اشارت به جوی های بهشت و آنچه در دوزخ بازاء آن بود .

فصل هفدهم: در اشارت به خازن بهشت و دوزخ و رسیدن مردم به فطرت اولی.

فصل هیجدهم: در اشارت به درخت طوبی و درخت زقّوم.

فصل نوزدهم: در اشارت به حور عین.

فصل بیستم: در اشارت به ثواب و عقاب [و عدل او] .

فصل اول
در صفت راه آخرت و ذکر سالکانش و اسباب اعراض مردم[۳۱] از آن و ذکر آفات آن[۳۲] اعراض

[§۴] بدانکه راه آخرت ظاهر است و راهبران آن معتمد و نشان های راه مکشوف و سلوکش آسان و لیکن مردم از آن مُعرضند: **وَكَأَيِّن مِّن آيَةٍ فِي السَّمَاوَاتِ وَالأَرْضِ يَمُرُّونَ عَلَيْهَا وَهُمْ عَنْهَا مُعْرِضُونَ**(۱۰۵:۱۲). اما سبب آسانی سلوك آنست که راه همان است که مردم از آنجا آمده اند، پس آنچه دیدنی است یك بار دیده اند و آنچه شنیدنی است یك بار شنیده اند ولیکن فراموش کرده اند: **وَلَقَدْ عَهِدْنَا إِلَى آدَمَ مِن قَبْلُ فَنَسِيَ وَلَمْ نَجِدْ لَهُ عَزْمًا**(۱۱۵:۲۰). <از این جهت>[۳۳] میگوید: **ارْجِعُوا وَرَاءكُمْ فَالْتَمِسُوا نُورًا** (۱۳:۵۷). و در فراموشی از آن بمانده اند که چشمی که بآن دیده اند و گوشی که بآن شنیده اند باز نمی کنند، تا حال[۳۴] بآن رسیده: **وَإِن تَدْعُوهُمْ إِلَى الْهُدَى لاَ يَسْمَعُواْ وَتَرَاهُمْ يَنظُرُونَ إِلَيْكَ وَهُمْ لاَ يُبْصِرُونَ**(۱۹۸:۷). چه اگر شنیدی شنیده ی اول و بدیدی دیده ی اول باز شناختی: من نظر اعتبر و من اعتبر عرف و اول الدین المعرفة.

[§۵] و اما سبب اعراض سه چیز است <چنانکه گفته اند>[۳۵] رؤساء[۳۶] الشیاطین ثلثه: یکی[۳۷] شوائب طبیعت مانند شهوت و غضب و توابع آن از حب مال و جاه و غیر آن: **تِلْكَ الدَّارُ الْآخِرَةُ نَجْعَلُهَا لِلَّذِينَ لَا يُرِيدُونَ عُلُوًّا فِي الْأَرْضِ وَلَا فَسَادًا وَالْعَاقِبَةُ لِلْمُتَّقِينَ**(۲۸:۸۳). دوم وساوس عادت مانند تسویلات نفس اماره و تزیینات[۳۸] اعمال غیر صالحه به سبب خیالات[۳۹] فاسده و اوهام کاذبه و لوازم آن از اخلاق رذیله و ملکات ذمیمه: **قُلْ هَلْ نُنَبِّئُكُمْ بِالْأَخْسَرِينَ أَعْمَالًا. الَّذِينَ ضَلَّ سَعْيُهُمْ فِي الْحَيَاةِ الدُّنْيَا وَهُمْ يَحْسَبُونَ أَنَّهُمْ يُحْسِنُونَ صُنْعًا**(۱۸:۱۰۳-۱۰۴)و سیم نوامیس[۴۰] امثله مانند متابعت[۴۱] غولان آدمی پیکر و تقلید جاهلان عالم نما[۴۲]<و اجابت استغواء و استهواء>[۴۳] شیاطین جن و انس و مغرور شدن به خداع و تلبیسات ایشان: **رَبَّنَا أَرِنَا الَّذَيْنِ أَضَلَّانَا مِنَ الْجِنِّ وَالْإِنسِ نَجْعَلْهُمَا تَحْتَ أَقْدَامِنَا لِيَكُونَا مِنَ الْأَسْفَلِينَ**(۴۱:۲۹).

[§۶] و ثمرهء اعراض این جهانی کوری[۴۴] آن جهان و شقاوت جاودانی باشد: **وَمَنْ أَعْرَضَ عَن ذِكْرِي فَإِنَّ لَهُ مَعِيشَةً ضَنكًا وَنَحْشُرُهُ يَوْمَ الْقِيَامَةِ أَعْمَى. قَالَ رَبِّ لِمَ حَشَرْتَنِي أَعْمَى وَقَدْ كُنتُ بَصِيرًا. قَالَ كَذَلِكَ أَتَتْكَ آيَاتُنَا فَنَسِيتَهَا وَكَذَلِكَ الْيَوْمَ تُنسَى**(۲۰:۱۲۴-۱۲۶). وکدام شقاوت بود <بالای آنکه>[۴۵] کسی بنزدیک خدای تعالی منسی باشد. و کوری در این موضع کوری دل است:[۴۶] **فَإِنَّهَا لَا تَعْمَى الْأَبْصَارُ وَلَكِن تَعْمَى الْقُلُوبُ الَّتِي فِي**

الصُّدُورِ (۴۶:۲۲) و آنرا مراتب است، ختم و طبع و رین: **خَتَمَ اللَّهُ عَلَى قُلُوبِهِمْ** (۷:۲) **بَلْ طَبَعَ اللَّهُ عَلَيْهَا بِكُفْرِهِمْ** (۱۵۵:۴) **كَلَّا بَلْ رَانَ عَلَى قُلُوبِهِم** (۱۴:۸۳) و این نهایت مراتب کوری است گر[۴۷] <چه مؤدی است>[۴۸] به حجاب بزرگتر: **كَلَّا إِنَّهُمْ عَن رَّبِّهِمْ يَوْمَئِذٍ لَّمَحْجُوبُونَ** (۱۵:۸۳). و بزرگترین آفات آنست که بیشتر کسان که مردمان ایشان را از زُمره[۴۹] راهبران می شمرند از راه بی خبرند: **يَعْلَمُونَ ظَاهِرًا مِّنَ الْحَيَاةِ الدُّنْيَا وَهُمْ عَنِ الْآخِرَةِ هُمْ غَافِلُونَ** (۷:۳۰). و متابعت ایشان إلا ضلالت نیفزاید: **وَإِن تُطِعْ أَكْثَرَ مَن فِي الْأَرْضِ يُضِلُّوكَ عَن سَبِيلِ اللَّهِ إِن يَتَّبِعُونَ إِلاَّ الظَّنَّ وَإِنْ هُمْ إِلاَّ يَخْرُصُونَ** (۶:۱۱۶).

[§۷] پس سبیل طالب سلوک جز اعتصام به حبل الهی که **وَاعْتَصِمُواْ بِحَبْلِ اللَّهِ جَمِيعًا**(۳:۱۰۳)، و تمسک به کلمات تامات زاکیه: **وَتَمَّتْ كَلِمَتُ رَبِّكَ صِدْقًا وَعَدْلاً لاَّ مُبَدِّلِ لِكَلِمَاتِهِ** (۶:۱۱۵) نیست. **وَكَفَى بِرَبِّكَ هَادِيًا وَنَصِيرًا** (۲۵:۳۱).

فصل دوم
در اشارت به مبدأ و معاد و آمدن از فطرت اولی و رسیدن به آنجا[۵۰] و ذکر شب قدر و روز قیامت

[§۸] مبدأ فطرت اولی[۵۱] است و معاد عود بآن فطرت: **فَأَقِمْ وَجْهَكَ لِلدِّينِ حَنِيفًا فِطْرَةَ اللَّهِ الَّتِي فَطَرَ النَّاسَ عَلَيْهَا لَا تَبْدِيلَ لِخَلْقِ اللَّهِ ذَٰلِكَ الدِّينُ الْقَيِّمُ** (۳۰:۳۰). <که اول>[۵۲] خدا بود و هیچ نه: کان الله و لم یکن معه شیءخلق را <از نیست>[۵۳] هست گردانید: **وَقَدْ خَلَقْتُكَ مِن قَبْلُ وَلَمْ تَكُ شَيْئًا** (۹:۱۹). وبآخر خلق نیست شوند و خدا هست[۵۴] بماند: **كُلُّ مَنْ عَلَيْهَا فَانٍ. وَيَبْقَىٰ وَجْهُ رَبِّكَ ذُو الْجَلَالِ وَالْإِكْرَامِ**(۵۵:۷-۲۶). پس چنانکه هست شدن خلق بعد از نیستی مبدأ خلق است، نیست شدن بعد از هستی معادشان باشد. چه آمدن و رفتن چون مقابل یکدیگرند <هریک عین دیگری>[۵۵] تواند بود: **كَمَا بَدَأْنَا أَوَّلَ خَلْقٍ نُّعِيدُهُ** (۲۱:۱۰۴). و از اینجا است که بحکم مبدأ خدا بگوید و خلق جواب دهند: **أَلَسْتُ بِرَبِّكُمْ قَالُواْ بَلَىٰ** (۷:۱۷۲) و بحکم معاد خدای بگوید و هم خدای جواب دهد: **لِّمَنِ الْمُلْكُ الْيَوْمَ لِلَّهِ الْوَاحِدِ الْقَهَّارِ** (۴۰:۱۶). وخلق چون اول از خدا وجود یافته اند، <نبوده اند پس هست شده اند>[۵۶] و بآخر وجود به خدای سپارند: **إِنَّ إِلَىٰ رَبِّكَ الرُّجْعَىٰ** (۹۶:۸)، پس نیست شوند: **كُلُّ شَيْءٍ هَالِكٌ إِلَّا وَجْهَهُ** (۲۸:۸۸). منه المبدأ و الیه المعاد.

[§۹] نیستی اول بهشتی[۵۷] است که آدم در آنجا بود: **اسْكُنْ أَنتَ وَزَوْجُكَ الْجَنَّةَ** (۱۹:۷)، و هستی بعد از نیستی آمدن بدنیا ست: **اهْبِطُواْ مِنْهَا جَمِيعاً** (۳۸:۲). و نیستی دوم که فنا در توحید است بهشتی است که <معاد موحدان بآنجا است:>[۵۸] **ارْجِعِي إِلَى رَبِّكِ رَاضِيَةً مَّرْضِيَّةً. فَادْخُلِي فِي عِبَادِي. وَادْخُلِي جَنَّتِي**(۸۹: ۳۰-۲۸). آمدن از بهشت به دنیا توجه از کمال به نقصان است و بیفتادن از فطرت اولی[۵۹] و لا محاله صدور خلق از خالق جز بر این نمط نتواند بود و رفتن از دنیا به بهشت توجه از نقصان به کمال است و رسیدن با فطرت اولی[۶۰] و لا محاله رجوع خلق با خالق جز بر این نسق[۶۱] صورت نبندد: **اللَّهُ يَبْدَأُ الْخَلْقَ ثُمَّ يُعِيدُهُ ثُمَّ إِلَيْهِ تُرْجَعُونَ** (۱۱:۳۰). پس اول نزول و هبوط است و دوم عروج و صعود. <اول افول نور دوم طلوع نور:>[۶۲] **اللَّهُ نُورُ السَّمَوَاتِ وَالأَرْضِ** (۳۵:۲۴). به این سبب عبارت از مبدأ به شب کرده اند و آن شب قدر است و عبارت از معاد به روز و آن روز قیامت است.

[§۱۰] در شب قدر: **تَنَزَّلُ الْمَلَائِكَةُ وَالرُّوحُ فِيهَا بِإِذْنِ رَبِّهِم مِّن كُلِّ أَمْرٍ** (۴:۹۷). < در روز قیامت: **تَعْرُجُ الْمَلَائِكَةُ وَالرُّوحُ إِلَيْهِ فِي يَوْمٍ**

كَانَ مِقْدَارُهُ خَمْسِينَ أَلْفَ سَنَةٍ (۴:۷۰).>[۶۳] وچون کمال مبدأ به[۶۴] معاد است، هم چنانکه کمال شب به روز است و کمال روز به ماه و کمال ماه به سال، پس[۶۵] اگر مبدأ شب قدر است معاد روز قیامت است و اگر شب قدر نسبت به ماه دارد: **لَيْلَةُ الْقَدْرِ خَيْرٌ مِّنْ أَلْفِ شَهْرٍ**<**تَنَزَّلُ الْمَلَائِكَةُ وَالرُّوحُ**>[۶۶] (۳:۹۷)، روز قیامت نسبت به سال دارد:>[۶۷] **يُدَبِّرُ الْأَمْرَ مِنَ السَّمَاءِ إِلَى الْأَرْضِ ثُمَّ يَعْرُجُ إِلَيْهِ فِي يَوْمٍ كَانَ مِقْدَارُهُ أَلْفَ سَنَةٍ** <**مِّمَّا تَعُدُّونَ** (۵:۳۲). و به وجهی>[۶۸] اگر مبدأ نسبت به روز دارد: خمرت طینة آدم بیدیّ اربعون صباحا،[۶۹] معاد نسبت به سال دارد که مابین النفختین اربعون عاما.[۷۰] و اگر شب قدر بر هزار ماه تفضیل دارد: **لَيْلَةُ الْقَدْرِ خَيْرٌ مِّنْ أَلْفِ شَهْرٍ** (۳:۹۷)، روز قیامت بقدر پنجاه هزار سال است: **فِي يَوْمٍ كَانَ مِقْدَارُهُ خَمْسِينَ أَلْفَ سَنَةٍ** < **فَاصْبِرْ صَبْرًا جَمِيلًا**>[۷۱](۷۰ :۵- ۴).

[§۱۱] موسی که مرد مبدأ است و صاحب تنزیل، صاحب غرب است که موضع[۷۲] اُفُول نور باشد: **وَمَا كُنتَ بِجَانِبِ الْغَرْبِيِّ إِذْ قَضَيْنَا إِلَى مُوسَى الْأَمْرَ** (۴۴:۲۸)، اول ما کتب الله تعالی التوریه.[۷۳] و عیسی که مرد[۷۴] معاد است و صاحب تأویل صاحب شرق است که موضع طُلوع نور باشد: **وَاذْكُرْ فِي الْكِتَابِ مَرْيَمَ إِذِ انتَبَذَتْ مِنْ أَهْلِهَا مَكَانًا شَرْقِيًّا** (۱۶:۱۹)، **وَإِنَّهُ لَعِلْمٌ لِّلسَّاعَةِ** (۶۱:۴۳). و محمد[۷۵] که جامع هر دو است

به وجهی متوسط است و به وجهی از هر دو مبرا . اما جامع، بحکم اینکه <هم در مبدأ>[۷۶] منزلتی دارد که کنت نبیا و آدم بین الماء والطین،[۷۷] لکل شی جوهر و جوهر الخلق محمد.[۷۸] و در معاد هم مرتبتی دارد که شفیع روز حشر است: ادخرت شفاعتی لاهل الکبائر من امتی.[۷۹] و اما متوسط به حکم آنکه از وسط عالم روی به مغرب باید کرد تا روی به قبلهء موسی باشد و به مشرق تا به قبلهء عیسی باشد و به میان هر دو تا قبلهء محمد[۸۰] باشد که مابین المشرق والمغرب قبلتی.[۸۱] وامّا از هر دو مبرا به حکم: إنه **لَّا شَرْقِيَّةٍ وَلَا غَرْبِيَّةٍ** (۳۵:۲۴) است: **إِنَّ فِي ذَٰلِكَ لَآيَاتٍ لِّقَوْمٍ يَتَفَكَّرُونَ** (۳:۱۳).

فصل سیم
در اشارت به هر دو جهان
و ذکر مراتب مردم در این جهان و در آن جهان

[§۱۲] خدای را تبارک و تعالی[۸۲] بحکم آنکه اول است و آخر (۳:۵۷) دو عالم است یکی دنیا و یکی آخرت؛ یکی این جهان و یکی آن جهان که این مبدأ است و آن معاد و به حکم آن که ظاهر و باطن

است دو عالم است، یکی عالم خلق و یکی عالم امر، یکی عالم ملک و یکی عالم ملکوت، یکی عالم غیب و یکی عالم شهادت که این محسوس است و آن معقول. و خلق را چون گذر بر این عالم ها است از دنیا به آخرت و از این جهان به آن جهان و از خلق به امر و از ملک به ملکوت و از غیب به شهادت[۸۳] رفتن ضرورت است. و انبیاء را بدین سبب فرستاده اند تا ایشان را از عالمی به عالمی خوانند چنانکه گفت منزَل بدان مقرر است. پس دعوت به إنباء[۸۴] است و نباء آن عالم است که خلق به آنجا میروند: **عَمَّ يَتَسَاءلُونَ عَنِ النَّبَإِ الْعَظِيمِ الَّذِي هُمْ فِيهِ مُخْتَلِفُونَ** (۷۸:۳-۱).

[§۱۳] خلق در دنیا در برزخ[۸۵] اند و برزخ سدی است ظلمانی متوسط میان مبدأ و معاد: **وَمِن وَرَائِهِم بَرْزَخٌ إِلَى يَوْمِ يُبْعَثُونَ** (۲۳:۱۰۰) و مردم اینجا بعضی خفته اند و بعضی مرده و خفتگان به حکم الدنیا مثل حُلم[۸۶] و مردگان به حکم: **أَمْواتٌ غَيْرُ أَحْيَاء** (۱۶:۲۱). **وَمَا أَنتَ بِمُسْمِعٍ مَّن فِي الْقُبُورِ** (۳۵:۲۲). هرکه از این زندگی بمُرد از خواب برخاست و قیامت برخاستن بود: فإذا ماتوا انتبهوا، من مات فقد قامت قیامته.[۸۷] و لیکن[۸۸] مرگ[۸۹] دو مرگ است یکی ارادی: موتوا قبل ان تموتوا[۹۰] و دیگری طبیعی: **أَيْنَمَا تَكُونُواْ يُدْرِككُّمُ الْمَوْتُ** (۴:۷۸). و هر که به مرگ ارادی بمیرد به زندگانی جاودانی زنده[۹۱] شود: مت بالاراده تحیی بالطبیعه[۹۲]

و هر که به مرگ طبیعی بمیرد[93] در ﴿هلاک جاودان افتد:﴾[94] ویل لمن انتبه بعد الموت.

[§۱۴] سرِّ قیامت سرّی بزرگ است، انبیاء را ﴿به کشف آن اجازه﴾[95] ندادند. چون انبیاء اصحاب شریعت اند، اصحاب قیامت دیگراند: إِنَّمَا أَنتَ مُنذِرٌ وَلِكُلِّ قَوْمٍ هَادٍ (۷:۱۳). محمد[96] علیه السلام[97] به قرب قیامت مخصوص است: أنا والساعة کهاتین،[98] حالش با قیامت آنست که يَسْأَلُونَكَ عَنِ السَّاعَةِ أَيَّانَ مُرْسَاهَا. فِيمَ أَنتَ مِن ذِكْرَاهَا. إِنَّمَا أَنتَ مُنذِرُ مَن يَخْشَاهَا (۴۳-۴۵:۷۹).

[§۱۵] قیامت روز ثواب است و شریعت روز عمل: الیوم عمل بلا ثواب و غدا ثواب بلا عمل. پیغمبران[99] در روز قیامت گواهان باشند: فَكَيْفَ إِذَا جِئْنَا مِن كُلِّ أُمَّةٍ بِشَهِيدٍ وَجِئْنَا بِكَ عَلَى هَٰؤُلَاءِ شَهِيدًا (۴۱:۴)، حاکم[100] قیامت دیگر[101] است: وَجِيءَ بِالنَّبِيِّينَ وَالشُّهَدَاءِ وَقُضِيَ بَيْنَهُم بِالْحَقِّ (۶۹:۳۹). شریعت راهست از شارع برگرفته اند و قیامت مقصد. صاحب شریعت میگوید بقیامت:[102] وَمَا أَدْرِي[103] مَا يُفْعَلُ بِي وَلَا بِكُمْ (۹:۴۶).

[§۱۶] خلق سالکان اند و تا اثری از مقصد به سالک[۱۰۴] نرسد سلوکش دست ندهد، و[۱۰۵] هیچ سالک تا از مقصد آگاه نشود بدان راغب نگردد و در حرکت نیاید. و آگاهی از مقصد معرفت و رغبت بدان محبت، پس[۱۰۶] تا عارف مُحِب نباشد او را سلوک دست ندهد. و[۱۰۷] معرفت و محبت اثر[۱۰۸] این[۱۰۹] وصول است و کمالش عین[۱۱۰] وصول و آنرا حشر خوانند: یحشر المرء من احب.

[§۱۷] و در آگاهی مراتب است چون ظن و علم و ابصار. ظن بوجهی این[۱۱۰] جهانی است و علم آن جهانی، به[۱۱۱] اینجا: **أَلَا إِنَّهُمْ فِي مِرْيَةٍ مِّن لِّقَائِه**(۵۴:۴۱) است و آنجا: **ثُمَ لَيَجْمَعَنَّكُمْ إِلَى يَوْمِ الْقِيَامَةِ لاَ رَيْبَ فِيهِ** (۸۷:۴).<و علم بوجهی این جهانی است و مشاهده و روئیت آن جهانی:>[۱۱۲] **كَلَّا لَوْ تَعْلَمُونَ عِلْمَ الْيَقِينِ، لَتَرَوُنَّ الْجَحِيمَ، ثُمَّ لَتَرَوُنَّهَا عَيْنَ الْيَقِينِ**<**ثُمَّ لَتُسْأَلُنَّ يَوْمَئِذٍ عَنِ النَّعِيمِ.**>(۱۰۲:۸-۵).[۱۱۳]

[§۱۸] اثر اول که از سلوک به سالک رسد ایمان است و اثر دوم ایقان[۱۱۴] به تحقیق آن < ایمان و تصدیق [به آن] باشد:>[۱۱۵] **إِنَّ هَذَا لَهُوَ حَقُّ الْيَقِينِ** (۹۵:۵۶) ایمان[۱۱۶] به آنچه در عالم غیب از آن محجوب اند: **يُؤْمِنُونَ بِاللهِ وَالْيَوْمِ الآخِرِ**(۱۱۴:۳) و ایقان[۱۱۷] به آنچه در عالم شهادت آنرا مشاهدند. پس ایمان نصیب اهل دنیا است: **يُؤْمِنُونَ بِالْغَيْبِ** (۳:۲)

و ایقان نصیب اهل آخرت: **وَبِالآخِرَةِ هُمْ يُوقِنُونَ** (۴:۲). اینجا: مِن اقل[۱۱۸] ما اوتیتم الیقین[۱۱۹] میگوید و دعوت به ایمان است: **آمِنُواْ بِرَبِّكُمْ** (۱۹۳:۳) و کمال ایمان به ایقان[۱۲۰] است: **وَاعْبُدْ رَبَّكَ حَتَّى يَأْتِيَكَ الْيَقِينُ** (۹۹:۱۵).

[§۱۹] ایمان را مراتب است، اول:[۱۲۱] **قَالَتِ الْأَعْرَابُ آمَنَّا قُل لَّمْ تُؤْمِنُوا وَلَكِن قُولُوا أَسْلَمْنَا وَلَمَّا يَدْخُلِ الْإِيمَانُ فِي قُلُوبِكُمْ** (۱۴:۴۹)، وسط:[۱۲۲] **وَقَلْبُهُ مُطْمَئِنٌّ بِالإِيمَانِ** (۱۰۶:۱۶)، آخر: **يَا أَيُّهَا الَّذِينَ آمَنُواْ آمِنُواْ**(۱۳۶:۴). پس ایمانی است بعد از ایمانی و: **إِذَا مَا اتَّقَواْ وَّآمَنُواْ وَعَمِلُواْ الصَّالِحَاتِ ثُمَّ اتَّقَواْ وَّآمَنُواْ**(۹۵:۵). و ایمان را نیز شرایط است: **فَلاَ وَرَبِّكَ لاَ يُؤْمِنُونَ حَتَّىَ يُحَكِّمُوكَ فِيمَا شَجَرَ بَيْنَهُمْ ثُمَّ لاَ يَجِدُواْ فِي أَنفُسِهِمْ حَرَجًا مِّمَّا قَضَيْتَ وَيُسَلِّمُواْ تَسْلِيمًا** (۶۵:۴). اول انقیاد فرمان ، بعد از آن رضا به قضا، بعد از آن تسلیم.

[§۲۰] ایقان را نیز مراتب است: **كَلَّا سَوْفَ تَعْلَمُونَ. ثُمَّ كَلَّا سَوْفَ تَعْلَمُونَ. كَلَّا لَوْ تَعْلَمُونَ عِلْمَ الْيَقِينِ. لَتَرَوُنَّ الْجَحِيمَ. ثُمَّ لَتَرَوُنَّهَا عَيْنَ الْيَقِينِ. ثُمَّ لَتُسْأَلُنَّ يَوْمَئِذٍ عَنِ النَّعِيمِ**(۱۰۲:۸-۳). مشاهده دوزخ بعد از حصول[۱۲۳] علم[۱۲۴] الیقین است و مشاهده بهشت[۱۲۵] بعد از حصول <عین الیقین>[۱۲۶]

چه باعلم [الیقین] هنوز حجاب باقی است به عین، و با عین [الیقین حجاب] باقی است به اثر.[۱۲۷]

[§۲۱] اهل گمان[۱۲۸] پندارند که قیامت هم به زمان[۱۲۹] دور است: **وَمَا أَظُنُّ السَّاعَةَ قَائِمَةً** (۳۶:۱۸) و <هم به مکان:>[۱۳۰] **وَيَقْذِفُونَ بِالْغَيْبِ مِن مَّكَانٍ بَعِيدٍ**(۵۳:۳۴) و اهل یقین[۱۳۱] دانند که هم به زمان نزدیک است: **اقْتَرَبَتِ السَّاعَةُ** (۱:۵۴) و هم به مکان: **وَأُخِذُوا مِن مَّكَانٍ قَرِيبٍ** (۵۱:۳۴)، إلا **إِنَّهُمْ يَرَوْنَهُ بَعِيدًا. وَنَرَاهُ قَرِيبًا** (۷۰:۷-۶). پیغمبر علیه السلام[۱۳۲] خود دست فراز[۱۳۳] کرد میوه بهشت برگرفت <و تا حارثه مشاهده این حال نکرد بر آنکه او مؤمن حقیقی است حکم نکرد.>[۱۳۴] إذ قال له "کیف اصبحت یا حارثه؟" قال "اصبحت مؤمناً حقاً،" قال علیه السلام "لکل حق حقیقة فما حقیقة ایمانک" قال "رأیت اهل الجنة یتزاورون و اهل النار یتعاورون و رأیت عرش ربی بارزا." فقال علیه السلام "اصبت فالزم"[۱۳۵] <ثم قال علیه السلام لأنس بن مالک "هذا شاب نور الله قلبه بالایمان.">[۱۳۶]

فصل چهارم
در اشارت به مکان و زمان آخرت

[§۲۲] دنیا چون ناقص است به مثابت کودک <و طفلان را >[۱۳۷] از دایه و گهواره <گریز نیست دایه او زمان است و گهواره او>[۱۳۸] مکان. و به وجهی پدر او زمان است و مادر او مکان. و زمان و مکان هریک به اثری از آثار مبدع خود مخصوص اند و آن <احاطت است به کائنات>[۱۳۹] چه <عین احاطت>[۱۴۰] خدای را است: **وَكَانَ اللّٰهُ بِكُلِّ شَيْءٍ مُّحِيطًا**(۴:۱۲۶).[۱۴۱] زمان را احاطت که اثر مبدع اوست چنان حاصل آید که بعضی < ازآن اول باشد>[۱۴۲] و بعضی آخر و مکان را چنان که بعضی ظاهر باشد[۱۴۳] و بعضی باطن و چون به ذات و به طبع[۱۴۴] نیستند هیچ کدام در هیچ کدام تمام[۱۴۵] نیست پس[۱۴۶] وجود هر[۱۴۷] بعضی از زمان اقتضاء عدم دیگر بعض می کند و حضور هر بعضی از مکان اقتضاء غیبت دیگر بعض.[۱۴۸] گذشته زمان نیست[۱۴۹] و آینده همچنین، اگر زمان وجودی دارد زمان حال است که کمترین زمانی است و از خردی مقدار ندارد و حکما آنرا آن خوانند. و اگر مکان را احاطتی هست همه مکان راست نه جزوی را <از او.>[۱۵۰] و همه زمان آن است که آسمان و زمین و دیگر کائنات را حاوی است.

[§۲۳] و آخرت از زمان و مکان مبرا است چه از نقصان منزه است اما نشانها که از آن به اهل زمان و مکان دهند گاه زمانی بود[۱۵۱] و گاه مکانی تا به لسان قومه بود. و نشان زمان کمترین زمانی تواند بود مانند حال: **وَمَا أَمْرُ السَّاعَةِ إِلاَّ كَلَمْحِ الْبَصَرِ أَوْ هُوَ أَقْرَبُ** (۱۶:۷۷)، و نشان مکان به فراخ ترین مکان: **وَجَنَّةٍ عَرْضُهَا كَعَرْضِ السَّمَاء وَالْأَرْضِ** (۵۷:۲۱). و ابداع هم زمانی نیست و صفت او به کمترین زمان کنند: <**وَمَا أَمْرُنَا إِلَّا وَاحِدَةٌ كَلَمْحٍ بِالْبَصَرِ**>[۱۵۷] (۵۴:۵۰). پس مبدأ و معاد از این روی متشابه اند. یقین که آخرتی است، تعلقش به زمان و مکان هم بر این سیاقت گیرد اما تعلق به قلت زمان[۱۵۱] چنانکه گفته اند: < الیقینیات لحظات>[۱۵۲]. و به وسعت مکان: **أَفَمَن شَرَحَ اللَّهُ صَدْرَهُ لِلْإِسْلَامِ فَهُوَ عَلَى نُورٍ مِّن رَّبِّهِ** (۳۹:۲۲).

فصل پنجم
در اشارت به حشر خلایق

[§۲۴] زمان علت تغیر است علی الاطلاق و مکان علت تکثر علی الاطلاق و تغیر و تکثر علت محجوب شدن بعضی از موجودات از بعضی. چون[۱۵۳] به قیامت مکان و زمان مرتفع شود و حجاب ها برخیزد وخلق[۱۵۴] اولین و آخرین مجتمع باشند. پس قیامت روز جمع است: **يَوْمَ**

يَجْمَعُكُمْ لِيَوْمِ الْجَمْعِ(۹:۶۴) و به وجهی روز فصل است چه دنیا کون مشابهت است، در وی حق و باطل مشابه نماید، متخاصمان در مقابل یکدیگر نشسته اند. آخرت کون مباینت است: **وَيَوْمَ تَقُومُ السَّاعَةُ يَوْمَئِذٍ يَتَفَرَّقُونَ** (۱۴:۳۰)، حق از باطل جدا کنند: **لِيَمِيزَ اللّهُ الْخَبِيثَ مِنَ الطَّيِّبِ** (۳۷:۸)، خصومت[۱۵۵] متخاصمان[۱۵۶] فصل کنند و به حقیقت حق و بطلان باطل حکم کنند: **لِّيَهْلِكَ مَنْ هَلَكَ عَن بَيِّنَةٍ وَيَحْيَى مَنْ حَيَّ عَن بَيِّنَةٍ** (۴۲:۸)، <**لِيُحِقَّ الْحَقَّ وَيُبْطِلَ الْبَاطِلَ**>(۸:۸)[۱۵۷] پس قیامت[۱۵۸] روز فصل است اما آن فصل اقتضای آن جمع می کند که در پیش بیامد: **هَذَا يَوْمُ الْفَصْلِ جَمَعْنَاكُمْ وَالْأَوَّلِينَ** (۳۸:۷۷). حشر جمع باشد، پس روز قیامت[۱۵۹] حشر است: **وَحَشَرْنَاهُمْ فَلَمْ نُغَادِرْ مِنْهُمْ أَحَدًا** (۴۷:۱۸).

[۲۵§] اما حشر ها متفاوت[۱۶۰] است قومی را چنین است[۱۶۱]: **يَوْمَ نَحْشُرُ الْمُتَّقِينَ إِلَى الرَّحْمَنِ وَفْدًا**(۸۵:۱۹)، و قومی را چنین: **وَيَوْمَ يُحْشَرُ أَعْدَاءُ اللَّهِ إِلَى النَّارِ**(۱۹:۴۱). و بر جمله حشر هرکسی به آنچه که سلوکش <در طلب آن بوده است:>[۱۶۲] حشره مع من یتولاه[۱۶۳] باشد. وبدین سبب: **احْشُرُوا الَّذِينَ ظَلَمُوا وَأَزْوَاجَهُمْ**(۲۲:۳۷) و همچنین: **فَوَرَبِّكَ لَنَحْشُرَنَّهُمْ وَالشَّيَاطِينَ**(۶۸:۱۹) تا به حدی که لواحب احدکم الحجر لنحشر معه.

[§۲۶] و چون آثار افعال مدبران برازخ حیوانی، چنانکه بعد از این گفته شود، مصور و حاضر کنند آن اصناف را جمله حشر کرده باشند: **وَإِذَا الْوُحُوشُ حُشِرَتْ** (۵:۸۱)، و حشر هر کسی بر صورت ذاتی آن کس تواند بود چه آنجا حجابها مرتفع است: **وَبَرَزُواْ للهِ الْوَاحِدِ الْقَهَّارِ**(۴۸:۱۴). بدین سبب یحشر بعض الناس علی صورة یحسن[۱۶۴] عندهم القرده و الخنازیر. و خود هم در این جهان: **وَجَعَلَ مِنْهُمُ الْقِرَدَةَ وَالْخَنَازِيرَ وَعَبَدَ الطَّاغُوتَ** (۶۳:۵) <و لیکن هم اینجا کسانی بیننده اهل آن جهان باشند:>[۱۶۵] **إِنَّ فِي ذَلِكَ لَآيَاتٍ لِّقَوْمٍ يَعْقِلُونَ** (۴:۱۳).

فصل ششم
در< اشارت به>[۱۶۶] احوال اصناف خلق در آن جهان و ذکر بهشت و دوزخ

[§۲۷] کسانی که در این عالم در معرض سلوک راه آخرت اند سه طایفه اند: **وَكُنتُمْ أَزْوَاجًا ثَلَاثَةً. فَأَصْحَابُ الْمَيْمَنَةِ مَا أَصْحَابُ الْمَيْمَنَةِ. وَأَصْحَابُ الْمَشْأَمَةِ مَا أَصْحَابُ الْمَشْأَمَةِ. وَالسَّابِقُونَ السَّابِقُونَ. أُوْلَئِكَ الْمُقَرَّبُونَ. فِي جَنَّاتِ النَّعِيمِ** (۷-۱۲:۵۶)، <و همچنین:>[۱۶۷] **فَمِنْهُمْ ظَالِمٌ لِّنَفْسِهِ وَمِنْهُم مُّقْتَصِدٌ وَمِنْهُمْ سَابِقٌ بِالْخَيْرَاتِ** (۳۲:۳۵).

[§۲۸] <سابقان اهل وحدت اند>[۱۶۸] از راه و از سلوک منزه، بل خود مقصد همه سالکان ایشانند: **وَلَا تَعْدُ عَيْنَاكَ عَنْهُمْ تُرِيدُ زِينَةَ الْحَيَاةِ الدُّنْيَا** (۲۸:۱۸). از ایشانند آن گروهی که إن حضروا لم یعرفوا وإن غابوا لم یفقدوا. و اهل یمین[۱۶۹] نیکان[۱۷۰] عالم اندو ایشان را مراتب بسیار است به حسب درجات بهشت و در ثواب متفاوت اند: **وَلِكُلٍّ دَرَجَاتٌ مِّمَّا عَمِلُوا** (۱۹:۴۶). واهل شمال بَدان عالم اند و ایشان را اگر چه مراتب است به حسب درکات[۱۷۱] دوزخ اما در عذاب متساوی اند: **قَالَ لِكُلٍّ ضِعْفٌ وَلَكِن لَّا تَعْلَمُونَ**(۳۸:۷)، و همچنین **فَإِنَّهُمْ يَوْمَئِذٍ فِي الْعَذَابِ مُشْتَرِكُونَ** (۳۳:۳۷).

[§۲۹] و هر سه طایفه را گذر بر دوزخ است: **وَإِن مِّنكُمْ إِلَّا وَارِدُهَا** <**كَانَ عَلَى رَبِّكَ حَتْمًا مَّقْضِيًّا**(۷۱:۱۹).>[۱۷۲] اما سابقان یمرون علی الصراط کالبرق الخاطف، ایشان را از دوزخ گریزی نیست. <"جزناها وهی خامدة">[۱۷۳]سخن یکی از امامان اهل بیت علیهم السلام است در جواب آنکه پرسید که "شما را گذر بر دوزخ چون[۱۷۴] باشد؟"

[§۳۰] و اما اهل یمین را از دوزخ نجات دهند و اهل شمال را آنجا بگذارند: **ثُمَّ نُنَجِّي الَّذِينَ اتَّقَوا وَّنَذَرُ الظَّالِمِينَ فِيهَا جِثِيًّا**(۷۲:۱۹). < سابقان

واهل یمین به بهشت رسند>[۱۷۵] اما کمال[۱۷۶] <بهشت به سابقان باشد:>[۱۷۷] إن الجنة اشوق إلی سلمان من سلمان إلی الجنة.[۱۷۸] ایشان را به بهشت التفات نبود: **لَمْ يَدْخُلُوهَا وَهُمْ يَطْمَعُونَ**(۷:۴۶)، وایشان اهل اعراف اند: **وَعَلَى الأَعْرَافِ رِجَالٌ يَعْرِفُونَ كُلاًّ بِسِيمَاهُمْ**(۷:۴۶)، ایشان را همه حالها یکسان باشد: **لِكَيْلَا تَأْسَوْا عَلَى مَا فَاتَكُمْ وَلَا تَفْرَحُوا بِمَا آتَاكُمْ** (۵۷:۲۳) وصف حال ایشان است.

[§۳۱] < اهل شمال>[۱۷۹] اهل تضادّ اند، باحوال متضادکه دراین عالم مقابل است مانند هستی و نیستی، مرگ و زندگی، علم و جهل، قدرت و عجز، لذت و الم و سعادت و شقاوت باز مانده اند. زیرا که <بخود باز مانده اند و از خود بخود>[۱۸۰] خلاص نتوانند یافت: **كُلَّمَا نَضِجَتْ جُلُودُهُمْ بَدَّلْنَاهُمْ جُلُودًا غَيْرَهَا لِيَذُوقُواْ الْعَذَابَ**(۴:۵۶).<لاجرم همیشه میان دو طرف سموم و زمهریر دوزخ متردد اند ، گاه بدین معذب[۱۸۱] و گاه بدان: **لَهُم مِّن فَوْقِهِمْ ظُلَلٌ مِّنَ النَّارِ وَمِن تَحْتِهِمْ ظُلَلٌ**(۳۹:۱۶).>[۱۸۲] چون بدنیا در ربقه طاعت که اول مرتبه است از مراتب ایمان نیامده[۱۸۳] اند و زمام اختیار بادست گرفته، بآخرت مجبور بمانده اند: **كُلَّمَا أَرَادُوا أَن يَخْرُجُوا مِنْهَا أُعِيدُوا فِيهَا** (۳۲:۲۰).

[§۳۲] و اهل یمین اهل ترتّب اند، همیشه در سلوک باشند تا کمالی بعد از کمالی ودرجه ئی بالای درجه ئی حاصل کنند: **لَهُمْ غُرَفٌ مِّن فَوْقِهَا غُرَفٌ**(۳۹:۲۰)؛ از عذاب اهل تضاد خلاص یافته اند: **وَلاَ خَوْفٌ عَلَيْهِمْ وَلاَ هُمْ يَحْزَنُونَ** (۲:۶۲). الحزن على ما فات والخوف بما لم يأت. چون به دنیا مجبور بوده اند: **وَمَا كَانَ لِمُؤْمِنٍ وَلَا مُؤْمِنَةٍ إِذَا قَضَى اللَّهُ وَرَسُولُهُ أَمْرًا أَن يَكُونَ لَهُمُ الْخِيَرَةُ مِنْ أَمْرِهِمْ**(۳۳:۳۶)، بآخرت[۱۸۴] مختار مطلق شده اند: **لَهُمْ فِيهَا مَا يَشَآؤُونَ**(۱۶:۳۱)[۱۸۵] تا به حکم عدل هریک را از جبر و اختیار نصیبی باشد.

[§۳۳] پس اگر این طایفه را به یکی از دو طرف تضاد ملابستی باشد آن تضاد نه تضاد حقیقی بود و ایشان بآن معاقب نباشند بل مثاب باشند. و آن مانند حرارت و برودت و زنجبیل و[۱۸۶] کافور باشد که غریزی[۱۸۷] اند، نه[۱۸۸] چون حرارت و برودت و زمهریر و سموم که غریب اند: **إِنَّ الْأَبْرَارَ يَشْرَبُونَ مِن كَأْسٍ كَانَ مِزَاجُهَا كَافُورًا**(۷۶:۵)، **وَيُسْقَوْنَ فِيهَا كَأْسًا كَانَ مِزَاجُهَا زَنجَبِيلًا**(۷۶:۱۷). همچنانکه منازعت اهل ترتب منازعتی مجازی باشد: **يَتَنَازَعُونَ فِيهَا كَأْسًا لَّا لَغْوٌ فِيهَا وَلَا تَأْثِيمٌ** (۵۲:۲۳)؛ تا لاجرم: <**وَنَزَعْنَا مَا فِي صُدُورِهِم مِّنْ غِلٍّ إِخْوَانًا عَلَى سُرُرٍ مُّتَقَابِلِينَ**(۱۵:۴۷). اما مخاصمت اهل تضاد مخاصمت حقیقی[۱۸۹] باشد: **إِنَّ ذَلِكَ لَحَقٌّ تَخَاصُمُ أَهْلِ النَّارِ**(۳۸:۶۴)؛ تا لاجرم:>[۱۹۰] **كُلَّمَا دَخَلَتْ أُمَّةٌ لَّعَنَتْ أُخْتَهَا** (۷:۳۸).[۱۹۱]

[§۳۴] پس حرارت و برودت که متضادند گاه هر دو[۱۹۲] طرف سبب عذاب قومی اند، چنانکه اهل دوزخ را، و گاه یک طرف سبب راحت قومی است و آن: **بَرْدًا وَسَلَامًا** (۶۹:۲۱) است.[۱۹۳] اهل برد [یعنی] المتقین را ، و دیگر طرف که نار است سبب عذاب کسانی که مقابل ایشان باشند.[۱۹۴] و گاه هر دو طرف سبب راحت قومی اند چنانکه در زنجبیل و کافور بگفتیم و همچنین[۱۹۵] عذاب قومی[۱۹۶] مانند نار الجحیم و گاه راحت قومی مانند آن نار که شخصی از قسیم الجنة والنار علیه السلام التماس کرد که یا قسیم النار"اجعلنی من اصحاب النار" تا او بخندید و بفرمود که "جعلتک" و بعد از آن با دیگر حاضران فرمود: "میخواهد که از اهل قیامت باشد."

[§۳۵] نیستی [را] هم اصناف است: نیستی قهر که به قیامت خاص و عام را باشد: **كُلُّ شَيْءٍ هَالِكٌ إِلَّا وَجْهَهُ** (۸۸:۲۸) و نیستی لطف که اهل وحدت را باشد: "من احبنی محوت اثره" نیستی عنف که اهل دوزخ را باشد: **لَا تُبْقِي وَلَا تَذَرُ**(۲۸:۷۴).

فصل هفتم
در< اشارت به >[۱۹۷] صراط

[§۳۶] صراط راه خدا است: **وَإِنَّكَ لَتَهۡدِيٓ إِلَىٰ صِرَٰطٖ مُّسۡتَقِيمٖ** (۵۲:۴۲). صراط الله الذی له ما فی السموات وما فی الارض، ادق من الشعر، احد من السیف. باریکی <به سبب>[۱۹۸] آنکه <اگر اندک>[۱۹۹] میلی <به یکی از>[۲۰۰] دو طرف تضاد افتد موجب هلاکت بود: **وَلَا تَرۡكَنُوٓاْ إِلَى ٱلَّذِينَ ظَلَمُواْ فَتَمَسَّكُمُ ٱلنَّارُ**(۱۱:۱۱۳). و تیزی به سبب آنکه مقام بر وی هم مقتضی هلاکت بود: ومن وقف علیها شقه بنصفین.

[§۳۷] دوزخیان از صراط به دوزخ افتند: **وَإِنَّ ٱلَّذِينَ لَا يُؤۡمِنُونَ بِٱلۡأٓخِرَةِ عَنِ ٱلصِّرَٰطِ لَنَٰكِبُونَ**(۲۳:۷۴)، از دو جانب صراط دوزخ است: الیمین والشمال مزلتان. بخلاف [۲۰۱]اعراف که الجنة علی یمینهم و <النار علی شمالهم>[۲۰۲] و اگر چه یمین و شمال[۲۰۳] ایشان همین باشد: <کلتا یدی الرحمن یمین.>[۲۰۴]

فصل هشتم
در اشارت به صحایف اعمال و کرام الکاتبین
و نزول ملائکه و شیاطین بر نیکان و بدان

[§۳۸] قول و فعل ما دام[۲۰۵] که در کون اصوات و حرکات باشد از بقا و ثبات بی نصیب باشد[۲۰۶] و چون به کون کتابت و تصویر آیند باقی و ثابت شوند. و ‹هر که قولی بگوید یا فعلی بکند اثری از آن باقی بماند.›[۲۰۷] و بدین سبب تکرار اقتضای اکتساب ملکه باشد که با وجود آن ملکه معاودت[۲۰۸] بآن قول یا فعل آسان بود.[۲۰۹] و اگر نه چنین بود هیچ کس[۲۱۰] علم و صناعت و حرفت نتوانستی آموخت و تأدیب کودکان و تکمیل ناقصان را فایده نبودی.

[§۳۹] پس آن اثرها که از اقوال و افعال ‹با مردم باقی بماند و بحقیقت بمثابت کتابت و تصویر آن افعال و اقوال باشد،›[۲۱۱] و محل آن کتابتها و تصویر ها را کتاب اقوال[۲۱۲] و صحیفه اعمال خوانند چه اقوال و افعال چون مشخص[۲۱۳] شوند کتابت باشد، چنانکه بیان کنیم إنشاء الله العزیز.[۲۱۴]

[§۴۰] و کاتبان و مصوران آن مکتوبات و مصورات کرام الکاتبین باشند. قومی[۲۱۵] که بر یمین باشند حسنات اهل یمین نویسند و قومی که بر شمال باشند سیئات اهل شمال نویسند: **إِذْ يَتَلَقَّى الْمُتَلَقِّيَانِ عَنِ الْيَمِينِ وَعَنِ الشِّمَالِ قَعِيدٌ**(۵۰:۱۷). در خبر است که هرکه حسنه کند از آن حسنه فرشته ئی در وجود آیدکه او را مثاب دارد. وهرکه سیئه کند <از آن سیئه>[۲۱۶] شیطانی در وجود آید که او را معذب دارد. وخود در قرآن مجید می گوید: **إِنَّ الَّذِينَ قَالُوا رَبُّنَا اللَّهُ ثُمَّ اسْتَقَامُوا تَتَنَزَّلُ عَلَيْهِمُ الْمَلَائِكَةُ أَلَّا تَخَافُوا وَلَا تَحْزَنُوا وَأَبْشِرُوا بِالْجَنَّةِ الَّتِي كُنتُمْ تُوعَدُونَ. نَحْنُ أَوْلِيَاؤُكُمْ فِي الْحَيَاةِ الدُّنْيَا وَفِي الْآخِرَةِ** (۴۱:۳۱-۳۰). و به مقابل: **هَلْ أُنَبِّئُكُمْ عَلَى مَن تَنَزَّلُ الشَّيَاطِينُ. تَنَزَّلُ عَلَى كُلِّ أَفَّاكٍ أَثِيمٍ** (۲۶:۲-۲۲۱)، و:[۲۱۷] **وَمَن يَعْشُ عَن ذِكْرِ الرَّحْمَٰنِ نُقَيِّضْ لَهُ شَيْطَانًا فَهُوَ لَهُ قَرِينٌ**(۴۳:۳۶).

[§۴۱] <همین است>[۲۱۸] که به عبارت اهل دانش ملکه[۲۱۹] گفته اند و به عبارت اهل بینش ملک[۲۲۰] و مقصود از هر دو یکی است و اگر نه مراد[۲۲۱] بقا و ثبات این ملکات بودی خلود ثواب و عقاب را بر اعمالی که در زمان اندک کرده باشند وجهی نبودی. ولکن حدیث[۲۲۲] إنما یخلد[۲۲۳] اهل الجنة فی الجنة واهل النار فی النار بالنیات <ثابت و وارد است.>[۲۲۴] پس هر که مثقال ذره نیکی کند یا بدی کند نیکی و بدی در کتاب مکتوب و مصوّر شود و مؤبد و مخلد بماند و چون پیش چشم

ایشان دارند که **وَإِذَا الصُّحُفُ نُشِرَتْ** (۸۱:۱۰)، کسانی که آن غافل مانده باشند گویند: **مَا لِهَٰذَا الْكِتَابِ لَا يُغَادِرُ صَغِيرَةً وَلَا كَبِيرَةً إِلَّا أَحْصَاهَا وَوَجَدُوا مَا عَمِلُوا حَاضِرًا وَلَا يَظْلِمُ رَبُّكَ أَحَدًا**(۱۸:۴۹).

[§۴۲] و[۲۲۵] در اخبار[۲۲۶] آمده است که < از گفتن>[۲۲۷] تسبیحی یا فعلی حسنه[۲۲۸] حوری بیافرینند که در بهشت جاودانی از آن تمتع یابند و در دیگر جانب[۲۲۹] همچنین باشد که در آن[۲۳۰] جهان از سیئات گناهکاران اشخاصی آفرینند که سبب محنت و عقوبت قومی شوند چنانکه در قصه پسر نوح آمده است: **إِنَّهُ عَمَلٌ غَيْرُ صَالِحٍ**(۱۱:۴۶). و در بنی اسرائیل: **وَلَقَدْ نَجَّيْنَا بَنِي إِسْرَائِيلَ**[۲۳۱] **مِنَ الْعَذَابِ الْمُهِينِ. مِن فِرْعَوْنَ إِنَّهُ كَانَ عَالِيًا مِّنَ الْمُسْرِفِينَ** (۴۴:۳۱-۳۰).

[§۴۳] در خبر است که "خلق الکافر من ذنب المؤمن"[۲۳۲] و امثال این بسیار است و این جمله به حکم آن باشد که **وَإِنَّ الدَّارَ الْآخِرَةَ لَهِيَ الْحَيَوَانُ لَوْ كَانُوا يَعْلَمُونَ**(۲۹:۶۴). پس هرچه در نظر اهل دنیا از ورای حجاب باشد آنرا غیر حیوان بینند و چون آن حجاب و غطا از پیش برگیرند حیات باشد: **فَكَشَفْنَا عَنكَ غِطَاءَكَ فَبَصَرُكَ الْيَوْمَ حَدِيدٌ**(۵۰:۲۲). و این آنگاه بود که از این حیات که به حقیقت مرگ است بمیرند و به حیات جاودانی[۲۳۳] آن جهانی که مرگ این جهانی است زنده شوند: **أَوَ مَن**

كَانَ مَيْتًا فَأَحْيَيْنَاهُ وَجَعَلْنَا لَهُ نُورًا يَمْشِي بِهِ فِي النَّاسِ كَمَن مَّثَلُهُ فِي الظُّلُمَاتِ لَيْسَ بِخَارِجٍ مِّنْهَا(۶:۱۲۲)، آنرا چنان بیند که باشد و اینست اجابت دعاء: "اللهم ارنا الأشیاء کما هی."[۲۳۴]

[§۴۴] پس هر کس را بعد از کشف غطا و حِدّت بصر کتاب خود باید خواند و حساب خود بکرد: **وَكُلَّ إِنسَانٍ أَلْزَمْنَاهُ طَائِرَهُ فِي عُنُقِهِ وَنُخْرِجُ لَهُ يَوْمَ الْقِيَامَةِ كِتَابًا يَلْقَاهُ مَنشُورًا. اقْرَأْ كَتَابَكَ كَفَى بِنَفْسِكَ الْيَوْمَ عَلَيْكَ حَسِيبًا**(۱۷:۱۴-۱۳). اگر سابق بالخیرات باشد یا از اهل یمین به حکم: "کما تعیشون تموتون و کما تموتون تبعثون" کتابش از پیش رو[۲۳۵] یا از جانب راستش بدو دهند: **فَأَمَّا مَن أُوتِيَ كِتَابَهُ بِيَمِينِهِ**، <**فَسَوفَ يُحاسَبُ حِساباً يَسِيراً**>[۲۳۶](۸۴:۸-۷). و اگر از جمله<منکوسان باشد:>[۲۳۷] **وَلَو تَرَى إِذِ اللمُجرِمُونَ نَاكِسُوا رُؤُسِهِم عِنَد رَبِّهِم**(۳۲:۱۲) و اگر از اهل شمال باشد کتابش را از وراء ظهر بدو دهند یا از جانب چپ: **وَأَمَّا مَنْ أُوتِيَ كِتَابَهُ وَرَاء ظَهْرِهِ** (۸۴:۱۰)، **وَأَمَّا مَنْ أُوتِيَ كِتَابَهُ بِشِمَالِهِ** (۶۹:۲۵).

فصل نهم
در اشارت به حساب و طبقات اهل حساب

[§۴۵] <در روز حساب>[۲۳۸] مردمان سه طایفه[۲۳۹] باشند، طایفه ئی: **يَدْخُلُونَ الْجَنَّةَ يُرْزَقُونَ فِيهَا بِغَيْرِ حِسَابٍ**(۴۰:۴۰)، و ایشان سه صنف[۲۴۰] باشند: صنف اول سابقان و اهل اعراف که از حساب منزه باشند. در خبر است که چون درویشان را به حسابگاه برند فرشتگان از ایشان حساب طلبند، گویند که بما چه داده اید که[۲۴۱] حساب باز دهیم. خطاب حضرت[۲۴۲]عزت در رسد که نیک میگویند شما را با حساب ایشان کار نیست. و خود خطاب با پیغامبر[۲۴۳] است[۲۴۴] در حق جماعتی که **مَا عَلَيْكَ مِنْ حِسَابِهِم مِّن شَيْءٍ وَمَا مِنْ حِسَابِكَ عَلَيْهِم مِّن شَيْءٍ**(۶:۵۲) و صنف دوم جماعتی از اهل یمین که بر سیئات اقدام نموده باشند: <**وَمَن تَقِ السَّيِّئَاتِ يَوْمَئِذٍ فَقَدْ رَحِمْتَهُ وَذَٰلِكَ هُوَ الْفَوْزُ الْعَظِيمُ**(۴۰:۹)>[۲۴۵] و صنف سیم جماعتی که <دیوان اعمال ایشان از سیئات[۲۴۶] خالی باشد.>[۲۴۷]

[§۴۶] اما [طایفه دوم از] اهل حساب نیز سه صنفند: صنف اول جماعتی که دیوان ایشان از حسنات خالی باشد. صنف دوم کسانی که **وَحَبِطَ مَا صَنَعُوا فِيهَا وَبَاطِلٌ مَّا كَانُوا يَعْمَلُونَ** (۱۱:۱۶) در شأن ایشان

است و [صنف سیم:] **وَقَدِمْنَا إِلَى مَا عَمِلُوا مِنْ عَمَلٍ فَجَعَلْنَاهُ هَبَاء مَّنثُورًا** (۲۳:۲۵).

[§۴۷] و طایفه سیم اهل حساب که **خَلَطُواْ عَمَلاً صَالِحًا وَآخَرَ سَيِّئًا**(۹:۱۰۲) و ایشان دو صنف باشند: صنفی که همیشه حساب خود میکنند: حاسبوا انفسکم قبل أن تحاسبوا[۲۴۸] شنیده اند، لاجرم به قیامت: **يُحَاسَبُ حِسَابًا يَسِيرًا**(۸:۸۴)؛ و صنفی که از حساب و کتاب غافل باشند لاجرم به مناقشات حساب مبتلا شوند: ومن نوقش فی الحساب <فقد عذب.>[۲۴۹]

[§۴۸] و حساب عبارت از حصر وجمع آثار حسنات و سیئاتی است که تقدیم یافته باشد تا به حکم عدل جزای هر یکی بیابند و موقنان همیشه مشاهد موقف حساب باشند: لا یؤخر حساب المؤمن الی یوم القیامه.[۲۵۰]

فصل دهم
در اشارت به وزن اعمال و ذکر[۲۵۱] میزان

[§۴۹] **وَالْوَزْنُ يَوْمَئِذٍ الْحَقُّ فَمَن ثَقُلَتْ مَوَازِينُهُ فَأُوْلَئِكَ هُمُ الْمُفْلِحُونَ. وَمَنْ خَفَّتْ مَوَازِينُهُ فَأُوْلَئِكَ الَّذِينَ خَسِرُواْ أَنفُسَهُم** (۷ :۸-۹). هر اثر فعل

که اقتضای اطمینان نفس فاعلی کند[۲۵۲] نسبت آن به ثقل اولی، چه مثقلات کشتی ها را از اضطراب و حرکت ناهموار نگهدارند. و هر حرکت[۲۵۳] که اقتضای تحیّر نفس و تتبع اهواء مختلف کند نسبتش به ‹خفت اولی،›[۲۵۴] چه خفیف به اندک تغیری که در هوا حادث شود در حرکت آید[۲۵۵] و حرکاتش از نظام خالی بود. و اطمینان نفس مستلزم رضا بود، لاجرم: **فَأَمَّا مَن ثَقُلَتْ مَوَازِينُهُ. فَهُوَ فِي عِيشَةٍ رَّاضِيَةٍ** (۱۰۱:۶-۷).

[§۵۰] اختلاف[۲۵۶] حرکات نفس اثر متابعت هوی، و هوی مؤدی باشد به هاویه، لاجرم: **وَأَمَّا مَنْ خَفَّتْ مَوَازِينُهُ. فَأُمُّهُ هَاوِيَةٌ. وَمَا أَدْرَاكَ مَا هِيَهْ. نَارٌ حَامِيَةٌ** (۱۰۱:۸-۱۱).

[§۵۱] و نیز ابلیس را از آتش آفریده اند و آدم را از خاک: **خَلَقْتَنِي مِن نَّارٍ وَخَلَقْتَهُ مِن طِينٍ** (۷:۱۲). وآتش خفیف است و خاک ثقیل، پس افعال ابلیس اقتضاء خفت کند و افعال آدمی اقتضاء ثقل، چه: **قُلْ كُلٌّ يَعْمَلُ عَلَى شَاكِلَتِهِ**(۱۷:۸۴).

[§۵۲] بعضی گفته اند کلمهء "لا اله الا الله" میزان است، هرچند فرموده اند: "کلمة خفیفة علی اللسان ثقیلة فی المیزان."[۲۵۷] اما نسبت با بعضی مردم موزون و میزان هردو یکی است و علامت آنکه این کلمه

میزان است آن است که وجود در یک کفه دارد <و عدم در یک کفه>[۲۵۸] و حرف استثنا که روئی با عدم دارد و روئی با وجود به مثابهء شاهین است که هر دو کفه به آن ایستاده <و قائم>[۲۵۹] است و این کلمه فاصل است میان مسلمان و کافر و بهشتی و دوزخی: من قال لااله الی الله دخل الجنة.[۲۶۰]

فصل یازدهم
در اشارت به طی آسمان ها

[§۵۳] کلام خدای تعالی دیگر است و کتاب خدا دیگر. کلام امری است و کتاب خلقی: **إِنَّمَا أَمْرُهُ إِذَا أَرَادَ شَيْئًا أَنْ يَقُولَ لَهُ كُنْ فَيَكُونُ** (۸۲:۳۶). وعالم امر از تضاد بل از تکثر منزه است: **وَمَا أَمْرُنَا إِلَّا وَاحِدَةٌ** (۵۰:۵۴). اما عالم خلق مشتمل بر تضاد و ترتب[۲۶۱] است: **وَلاَ رَطْبٍ وَلاَ يَابِسٍ إِلاَّ فِي كِتَابٍ مُّبِينٍ**(۵۹:۶).

[§۵۴] همچنانکه کلام مشتمل است برآیات: **تِلْكَ آيَاتُ اللهِ نَتْلُوهَا عَلَيْكَ بِالْحَقِّ**(۲۵۲:۲)، کتاب هم مشتمل است برآیات: **تِلْكَ آيَاتُ الْكِتَابِ الْمُبِينِ** (۲:۲۸). کلام چون مشخص[۲۶۲]شود کتاب باشد،

<چنانکه چون>[۲۶۳] امر امضا یابد فعل باشد: **كُنْ فَيَكُونُ** (۸۲:۳۶). پس صحیفه[۲۶۴] وجود عالم خلق کتاب خدای است <جل جلاله>[۲۶۵] و آیات او[۲۶۶] اعیان موجودات: **إِنَّ فِي اخْتِلاَفِ اللَّيْلِ وَالنَّهَارِ وَمَا خَلَقَ اللّهُ فِي السَّمَاوَاتِ وَالأَرْضِ لآيَاتٍ لِّقَوْمٍ يَتَّقُونَ**(۶:۱۰). و این[۲۶۷] آیات در آن کتاب مثبت و مبین است <تا خلق به مطالعه آیات فعلی که در آفاق مثبت است و استماع آیات قولی که از انفس مبین است بحق رسند:>[۲۶۸] **سَنُرِيهِمْ آيَاتِنَا فِي الْآفَاقِ وَفِي أَنفُسِهِمْ حَتَّى يَتَبَيَّنَ لَهُمْ أَنَّهُ الْحَقُّ**(۵۳:۴۱).

[§۵۵] و مردم تا در تحت زمان و مکان اند آن آیات برو می خوانند و باو[۲۶۹] می نمایند یکی بعد از دیگری و آن روزی است بعد روزی که بر او میگذرد و حالی بعد حالی که مشاهده میکند: **وَذَكِّرْهُمْ بِأَيَّامِ اللّهِ إِنَّ فِي ذَلِكَ لآيَاتٍ**(۵:۱۴)؛ برمثال کسی که نامه ئی می خواند، سطری بعد سطری و حرفی بعد حرفی. پس چون نظر بصیرت او بکحل هدایت گشوده شود، چنانکه اهل قیامت را <گفته اند>[۲۷۰] از عالم خلق بگذرد و به عالم امر رسد، که مبدأش از آنجا بوده است، برهمهء کتاب به یک بار مطلع گردد. مانند کسی که نامه ئی مشتمل بر سطور و حروف به یک بار در پیچیده پیش او باشد: **يَوْمَ نَطْوِي السَّمَاء كَطَيِّ السِّجِلِّ لِلْكُتُبِ** (۱۰۴:۲۱)؛ **وَالسَّماوَاتُ مَطْوِيَّاتٌ بِيَمِينِهِ**(۶۷:۳۹). نمی گوید بشماله تا

دانند که اهل شمال را از طی آسمانها نصیبی نیست. و اگر به خود قدرت مطالعه نداشته باشند و چون بر او خوانند استماع نکند[۲۷۱] حالش این بود که **يَسْمَعُ آيَاتِ اللَّهِ تُتْلَى عَلَيْهِ ثُمَّ يُصِرُّ مُسْتَكْبِرًا كَأَن لَّمْ يَسْمَعْهَا فَبَشِّرْهُ بِعَذَابٍ أَلِيمٍ**(۸:۴۵). و در سمع و بصر و کلام و کتاب اسرار بسیار است که ذکر آن در این مختصر ممکن نباشد.

فصل دوازدهم
در اشارت به نفخات صور و تبدیل زمین و آسمان

[§۵۶] نفخهء صور در قیامت دو نفخه است: اول از جهت اِماتت؛ هرکه پندارد که حیاتی دارد از اهل آسمانها و زمین که اصحاب ظاهر تنزیل و باطن تأویل اند، یا بر محسوس و معقول، خود تأویلی[۲۷۲] کرده آید: **وَنُفِخَ فِي الصُّورِ فَصَعِقَ مَن فِي السَّمَاوَاتِ وَمَن فِي الْأَرْضِ إِلَّا مَن شَاءَ اللَّهُ** (۶۸:۳۹).

[§۵۷] اماتت ایشان کشف<عوارت مقالات و کسر آراء دیانات>[۲۷۳] ایشان باشد تا به معاینه نیستی خود در دانش و بینش بدانند و به حقیقت: **إِنَّكُمْ وَمَا تَعْبُدُونَ مِن دُونِ اللَّهِ حَصَبُ جَهَنَّمَ أَنتُمْ لَهَا وَارِدُونَ**

(۹۸:۲۱) متیقن شوند؛ **وَإِذَا وَقَعَ الْقَوْلُ عَلَيْهِمْ أَخْرَجْنَا لَهُمْ دَابَّةً مِّنَ الْأَرْضِ تُكَلِّمُهُمْ أَنَّ النَّاسَ كَانُوا بِآيَاتِنَا لَا يُوقِنُونَ**(۸۲:۲۷).

[§۵۸] و نفخهء دوم از جهت احیاء ایشان بعد از اماتت و قیام از خواب جهالت: **ثُمَّ نُفِخَ فِيهِ أُخْرَى فَإِذَا هُم قِيَامٌ يَنظُرُونَ**(۶۸:۳۹). و آن قیام قیامت باشد و روز قیامت بعث بود: **ثُمَّ إِنَّكُمْ يَوْمَ الْقِيَامَةِ تُبْعَثُونَ** (۱۶:۲۳). پس ثواب و عقاب <باشد و>[۲۷۴] کسانی باشند که دنیا و آخرت ایشان متحد شده باشد: "لو کشف الغطاء ما ازددت یقینا،"[۲۷۵] به آن محتاج نباشند: **فَكَشَفْنَا عَنكَ غِطَاءَكَ فَبَصَرُكَ الْيَوْمَ حَدِيدٌ**(۲۲:۵۰). پس عمل و ثواب ایشان هم یکی باشد: "أعبد الله لا لرغبه و لا لرهبه بل إنه اهل لأن یعبد،"[۲۷۶] پس ایشان را انتظار قیامت و بعث و ثواب نباشد.

[§۵۹] و غیر ایشان را در نشأة ثانیه مکشوف شود که هستی ایشان نیستی بوده است و نیستی هستی، و ذات ایشان بی ذاتی و بی ذاتی ذات، وصفت ایشان بی صفتی و بی صفتی صفت. پس بینند که ظاهر چیز ها نه آن است که ایشان بظاهر داشته اند و بواطن و حقایق نه آنکه ایشان بواطن و حقیقت داشته اند و از ارتفاع حجب ظاهر و باطن به حقیقت حقایق ذات و ذوات برسند. پس زمین نه آن زمین بود که در

نشأة اولی آن را زمین میدانسته اند و آسمان نه آن آسمان بود که **يَوْمَ تُبَدَّلُ الأَرْضُ غَيْرَ الأَرْضِ وَالسَّمَاوَاتُ وَبَرَزُواْ للهِ الْوَاحِدِ الْقَهَّارِ**(۴۸:۱۴).

فصل سیزدهم
در اشارت به حالها که در روز قیامت حادث شوند و وقوف خلق به عرصات

[۶۰§] آفتاب مفیض انوار کلی است در آفرینش این عالم و ماه از آن استفاضت نور می کند و بر مادون خود افاضت می کند در وقت غیبت او. و کواکب مبادی فیضان انوار جزوی اند. چون نورالانوار مکشوف شود کواکب را وجود نماند: **وَإِذَا الكَوَاكِبُ انتَثَرَتْ** (۲:۸۲)؛ و ماه محو شود: **وَخَسَفَ الْقَمَرُ**(۸:۷۵) و مستفیض به مفیض پیوندد: **وَجُمِعَ الشَّمْسُ وَالْقَمَرُ** (۹:۷۵). وچون ذوالنور و نور یکی شود نه از افاضت اثری ماند و نه از استفاضت: **إِذَا الشَّمْسُ كُوِّرَتْ** (۱:۸۱)؛ **لَا يَرَوْنَ فِيهَا شَمْسًا وَلَا زَمْهَرِيرًا** (۱۳:۷۶).

[۶۱§] جبال را که مقتضی اعوجاج طرق وصول و مقتضی مقاسات تعب[۲۷۷] سلوک است به اول: **كَالْعِهْنِ الْمَنفُوشِ** (۵:۱۰۱) کنند و آخر

بکلی نسف کنند: **وَيَسْأَلُونَكَ عَنِ الْجِبَالِ فَقُلْ يَنسِفُهَا رَبِّي نَسْفًا. فَيَذَرُهَا قَاعًا صَفْصَفًا. لَا تَرَى فِيهَا عِوَجًا وَلَا أَمْتًا** (۲۰:۷-۱۰۵)، یعنی <تشبیه و تنزیه>.[۲۷۸]

[§۶۲] <و بحار را>[۲۷۹] که عبور از آن – جز بواسطه کشتیها که رساننده است به ساحل نجات و استدلال به ثواقب کواکب – متعذر باشد از میان بر گیرند: **وَإِذَا الْبِحَارُ سُجِّرَتْ** (۸۱:۶). تا بحر و بر، شیب و بالا و آسمان و زمین یکسان شوند و خلایق به عرصات قیامت ظاهر شوند: **فَإِذَا هُم بِالسَّاهِرَةِ** (۷۹:۱۴). اهل[۲۸۰] برازخ را حجب رقیق و کثیف از پیش بردارند: **وَإِذَا الْقُبُورُ بُعْثِرَتْ**(۸۲:۴) و در مواقف کشف اسرار بدارند: **وَقِفُوهُمْ إِنَّهُم مَّسْئُولُونَ** (۳۷:۲۴).

[§۶۳] آنها که از حبس برزخ خلاص یابند روی به بارگاه ربوبیت نهند: **فَإِذَا هُم مِّنَ الْأَجْدَاثِ إِلَى رَبِّهِمْ يَنسِلُونَ** (۳۶:۵۱). سموم و انیاب و اظفار <و قرون>[۲۸۱] از هوام و سباع باز ستانند تا سورت اطراف تضاد شکسته شود؛ يؤخذ السّم من الصل والناب من الذئب والقرن من الكبش: **لَا يَرَوْنَ فِيهَا شَمْسًا وَلَا زَمْهَرِيرًا** (۷۶:۱۳).

[§۶٤] و مرگ را که به هردو طرف تضاد سبب هلاک خلق بود بر صورت کبشی املح میان بهشت و دوزخ بکُشَند تا به مرگ مرگ، که نیستی نیستی باشد، هستی مطلق که حیات ابدی باشد عیان شود و دوزخ را ‹به صورت›[۲۸۲] شتری به عرصات آرند: **وَجِيءَ يَوْمَئِذٍ بِجَهَنَّمَ** (۲۳:۸۹) تا اهل عیان او را مشاهده کنند: **وَبُرِّزَتِ الْجَحِيمُ لِمَن يَرَى** (۳۶:۷۹) و از هول مشاهده او اجزای آفرینش بر نیستی خود اطلاع یابند: فشرد شرده لولا ان حبسها الله لأحترقت السموات والأرض.[۲۸۳]

فصل چهاردهم
در اشارت به درهای بهشت و دوزخ

[§۶۵] مشاعر حیوانی که بدان اجزای عالم مُلک ادراک کنند هفت است، پنج ظاهر و آن حواس خمسه[۲۸۴] است و دو باطن و آن خیال و وهم است که یکی مدرک صور[۲۸۵] و یکی مدرک معانی است، چه مفکره و حافظه و ذاکره از مشاعر نیستند بل اعوان ایشانند. و برای[۲۸۶] هر نفس که متابعت هوی کند و عقل را در متابعت هوی مسخر گرداند: **أَفَرَأَيْتَ مَنِ اتَّخَذَ إِلَهَهُ هَوَاهُ** (۲۳:۴۵)، هریکی از این مشاعر سببی باشند از اسباب هلاک: **وَأَضَلَّهُ اللَّهُ عَلَى عِلْمٍ** (۲۳:۴۵). تا

حالش آن بود که **فَأَمَّا مَن طَغَى. وَآثَرَ الْحَيَاةَ الدُّنْيَا. فَإِنَّ الْجَحِيمَ هِيَ الْمَأْوَى** (۷۹:۹-۳۷). پس هر یک از این مشاعر دری از درهای دوزخ است: **لَهَا سَبْعَةُ أَبْوَابٍ لِّكُلِّ بَابٍ مِّنْهُمْ جُزْءٌ مَّقْسُومٌ** (۱۵:۴۴).

[§۶۶] و اگر عقل که مدرک عالم ملکوت است و رئیس آن مشاعر، رئیسی مطاع باشد، تا به هر یکی از آن مشاعر مطالعه کتاب الهی در کتاب خلقی که ادراکش بدان مشعر[۲۸۷] خاص باشد به تقدیم رساند و به عقل نیز استماع آیات کلام الهی از عالم امری[۲۸۸] تلقی کند و به خلاف آن قوم: **وَقَالُوا لَوْ كُنَّا نَسْمَعُ أَوْ نَعْقِلُ مَا كُنَّا فِي أَصْحَابِ السَّعِيرِ**(۶۷:۱۰)، این مشاعر هشتگانه که عقل– با هفت حس مدرک که مذکور شد باشد – به مثابت در های بهشت باشند: **وَأَمَّا مَنْ خَافَ مَقَامَ رَبِّهِ وَنَهَى النَّفْسَ عَنِ الْهَوَى. فَإِنَّ الْجَنَّةَ هِيَ الْمَأْوَى** (۷۹:۴۱-۴۰).

فصل پانزدهم
در اشارت به زبانیهء دوزخ

[§۶۷] مدبران امور برازخ علوی که **وَالسَّابِحَاتِ سَبْحًا. فَالسَّابِقَاتِ سَبْقًا. فَالْمُدَبِّرَاتِ أَمْرًا**(۷۹:۵-۳) اشارت به احوال ایشان است هفت ستاره اند که در دوازده میدان[۲۸۹] سیر میکنند و مجموع هفت و دوازده نوزده

باشد. و مباشران امر در برازخ سفلی هم نوزده اند؛ هفت مبدأ قوای نباتی است، سه اصل <نامیه و مصوره و مولده>[۲۹۰] و چهار فرع <جاذبه و ماسکه و هاضمه و دافعه>[۲۹۱] و دوازده مبدأ قوای حیوانی است. ده مبادی احساس که از آن پنج ظاهر است و پنج باطن <ظاهر مشهور است و پنج باطن اول حس مشترک و وهم و قوت متخیله و قوت حافظه و ذاکره>[۲۹۲] و دو مبادی تحریک[۲۹۳] که یکی قوت جذب است و دیگر قوت دفع و مجموع نوزده باشد.

[§۶۸] پس مردم مادام تا در سجن دنیا محبوس اند اسیر تأثیر این نوزده کارکن از علوی و نوزده کارکن از سفلی اند. اگر از این منزل برنگذرد[۲۹۴] لامحاله "کما تعیشون تموتون و کما تموتون تبعثون"[۲۹۵] پس چون از سجن به سجین رسد او را مالک جهنم به این نوزده زبانیه که از آثار تعلق یکی از آن دو نوزده، چنانکه گفته شد، به او پیوسته باشد معذب دارند: **عَلَيْهَا تِسْعَةَ عَشَرَ** (۷۴:۳۰).

[§۶۹] مگر که بر صراط مستقیم که **وَأَنَّ هَذَا صِرَاطِي مُسْتَقِيمًا فَاتَّبِعُوهُ وَلاَ تَتَّبِعُواْ السُّبُلَ فَتَفَرَّقَ بِكُمْ عَن سَبِيلِهِ** (۶:۱۵۳) بگذرد تا به نور هدایت هادی قیامت[۲۹۶] به دارالسلام رسد و از این نوزده زبانیه خلاص یابد:

ضَرَبَ اللَّهُ مَثَلًا رَّجُلًا فِيهِ شُرَكَاء مُتَشَاكِسُونَ وَرَجُلًا سَلَمًا لِّرَجُلٍ هَلْ يَسْتَوِيَانِ مَثَلًا الْحَمْدُ لِلَّهِ بَلْ أَكْثَرُهُمْ لَا يَعْلَمُونَ (۲۹:۳۹).

فصل شانزدهم
در اشارت به جوی های بهشت
و آنچه در دوزخ به ازای آن بود

[§۷۰] آب ماده حیات کافهء اصناف نباتات و حیوانات است: **وَجَعَلْنَا مِنَ الْمَاء كُلَّ شَيْءٍ حَيٍّ** (۲۱:۳۰) مانند مواعظ و نصایحی که عموم مردم را به آن انتفاع باشد. و لیکن[۲۹۷] بعضی از آن اجاج است و بعضی آسن و بعضی غیر آسن. و بهترین غیر آسن است.

[§۷۱] شیر ماده تربیت اصناف حیوانات است و از آب خاص تر است چه نبات و بهری حیوانات را از آن نصیب نباشد و خاص غذای بعضی از حیوانات <بود در ایام طفولیت مانند مبادی و ظواهر>[۲۹۸] علوم که سبب ارشاد مبتدیان باشد. وآن نیز بعضی مستحیل و بعضی متغیر و بعضی غیر متغیر باشد. <و بهترین غیر متغیر باشد.>[۲۹۹]

[§۷۲] < و عسل از شیر خاص تر است>[۳۰۰] که غذای بعضی از حیوانات است و سبب شفاء بعضی اصناف در بعضی احوال و موافق همهء امزجه و احوال نیست. مانند حقایق و غوامض علوم که انتفاع بدان خاص الخواص و محققان را باشد و از آن نیز بعضی کَدَر است و بعضی متوسط و بعضی مُصفا <و بهترین مصفا است.>[۳۰۱]

[§۷۳] و خَمر از عسل خاص تر است چه خاص نوع انسان است و از ایشان به بعضی اصناف در بعضی احوال بر اهل دنیا حرام است و ایشان را رجس، و بر اهل بهشت حلال و ایشان را طَهور. و از آن بعضی مؤذی است و بعضی متوسط و بعضی مُلِذ. وبهترین آن ملذ است و طَهور.

[§۷۴] پس آب سبب خلاص است از تشنگی و شیر از نقصان و عسل از بیماری و خمر از اندوه و چون اهل بهشت اهل کمالند تمتع ایشان عام است از این هر چهار <بر وجه اتم،>[۳۰۲] چه آنچه ناقص را بدان انتفاع باشد کامل را نیز انتفاع بود و لا ینعکس: **مَثَلُ الْجَنَّةِ الَّتِي وُعِدَ الْمُتَّقُونَ فِيهَا أَنْهَارٌ مِّن مَّاء غَيْرِ آسِنٍ وَأَنْهَارٌ مِن لَّبَنٍ لَّمْ يَتَغَيَّرْ طَعْمُهُ وَأَنْهَارٌ مِّنْ خَمْرٍ لَّذَّةٍ لِّلشَّارِبِينَ وَأَنْهَارٌ مِّنْ عَسَلٍ مُّصَفًّى وَلَهُمْ فِيهَا مِن كُلِّ الثَّمَرَاتِ** (۱۵:۴۷).

[§۷۵] اما ثمرات بهشت در نظر اهل دنیا متشابه نماید، <فکیف آنچه در تحت هر یکی باشد>[۳۰۳] زیرا که اینجا حق و باطل متشابهند: **وَأُتُواْ بِهِ مُتَشَابِهاً** (۲۵:۲) و در دوزخ بازاء این چهار نهر، حمیم و غسلین و قطران و مهل باشد: **وَتِلکَ الأمثالُ نَضرِبُها لِلنّاسِ وَمايَعقِلُها إلّا العالِمُونَ**(۴۳:۲۹).

فصل هفدهم
در اشارت به خازن بهشت و دوزخ و رسیدن مردم به فطرت اولی[۳۰۴]

[§۷۶] در نشأت اولی به ابتدا مردم را وجود داده اند پس آگاهی پس قدرت پس ارادت، چه به اول یک چندی موجود بوده اند در صورت[۳۰۵] سلاله و نطفه و علقه و مضغه و عظام و لحم تا بعد از آن زنده و خبر دار شدند:[۳۰۶] **هَلْ أَتَى عَلَى الْإِنسَانِ حِينٌ مِّنَ الدَّهْرِ لَمْ يَكُن شَيْئًا مَّذْكُورًا** (۷۶:۱). و یک چندی زنده بود تا قوت حرکت و نطق[۳۰۷] در او ظهور کرد و یک چند متحرک بود تا قوت تمییز میان نافع و ضار در او به فعل آمد و بعد از آن[۳۰۸] مرید نافع و کارِه ضار گشت.

[§۷۷] و چون معاد عود است با فطرت اول، میباید که آن صفات در وی منتفی شود بر عکس این ترتیب. پس اول باید که ارادتش در ارادت واحد مطلق که موجد[۳۰۹] کل است مستغرق و منتفی شود چنانکه او را هیچ ارادت نماند. و چون وجود[۳۱۰] تابع ارادت واحد مطلق است، تعالی ذکره، پس هر چه آید مطابق ارادت او باشد و این درجهء رضا است و صاحب این درجه همیشه در بهشت بود: **لَهُم مَّا يَشَاؤُونَ فِيهَا وَلَدَيْنَا مَزِيدٌ** (۵۰:۳۵). و به این سبب خازن بهشت را رضوان خوانند، چه تا به این مقام نرسند از نعیم بهشت لذت نیابند: **وَرِضْوَانٌ مِّنَ اللّهِ أَكْبَرُ** (۹:۷۲).

[§۷۸] و بعد از آن باید که قدرتش در قدرت او تعالی منتفی شود تا قدرت خود را به هیچ [وجه] مغایر قدرت او نداند و این مرتبه را توکل خوانند: **وَمَن يَتَوَكَّلْ عَلَى اللَّهِ فَهُوَ حَسْبُهُ إِنَّ اللَّهَ بَالِغُ أَمْرِهِ قَدْ جَعَلَ اللَّهُ لِكُلِّ شَيْءٍ قَدْرًا** (۶۵:۳).

[§۷۹] و بعد از آن باید که علمش در علم او تعالی منتفی شود تا به خودی خود هیچ نداند و این مرتبه را تسلیم خوانند: **وَيُسَلِّمُواْ تَسْلِيمًا** (۴:۶۵).

[§۸۰] و بعد از آن باید که وجودش در وجود او تعالی منتفی شود تا به خود هیچ نباشد و این مقام اهل وحدت است: **أُوْلَئِكَ الَّذِينَ أَنْعَمَ اللَّهُ عَلَيْهِم مِّنَ النَّبِيِّينَ** (۵۸:۱۹).

[§۸۱] و اگر سالک این طریق نسپرد [یعنی به درجه رضا نائل نشود] و بر حسب ارادت[۳۱۱] خود رود، ارادت او هواهای مختلف مخالف حق اقتضا کند: **وَلَوِ اتَّبَعَ الْحَقُّ أَهْوَاءهُمْ لَفَسَدَتِ السَّمَاوَاتُ وَالْأَرْضُ وَمَن فِيهِنَّ** (۷۱:۲۳)، پس از هوای خود ممنوع نشود:[۳۱۲] **وَحِيلَ بَيْنَهُمْ وَبَيْنَ مَا يَشْتَهُونَ** (۵۴:۳۴)، در سخط خدای تعالی افتد: **أَفَمَنِ اتَّبَعَ رِضْوَانَ اللَّهِ كَمَن بَاء بِسَخْطٍ مِّنَ اللَّهِ** (۱۶۲:۳). هوی او را به هاویه رساند تا به اغلال و سلاسل نامرادی کلی[۳۱۳] مغلول و مقید گردد. و نامرادی وصف ممالیک است، به این سبب خازن هاویه را مالک خوانند.

[§۸۲] <و بعد از این>[۳۱۴] به ازاء درجهٔ توکل درکهٔ خذلان باشد: **وَإِن يَخْذُلْكُمْ فَمَن ذَا الَّذِي يَنصُرُكُم مِّن بَعْدِهِ** (۱۶۰:۳). و به ازاء درجهٔ تسلیم درکهٔ هوان بود: **وَمَن يُهِنِ اللَّهُ فَمَا لَهُ مِن مُّكْرِمٍ** (۱۸:۲۲). و به ازاء درجه وحدت درکهٔ لعنت: **أُولَئِكَ يَلعَنُهُمُ اللَّهُ وَيَلْعَنُهُمُ اللَّاعِنُونَ** (۱۵۹:۲). تا هم چنانکه انتفاء[۳۱۵] قدرت و علم و وجود طایفهٔ اول اقتضای قدرت نامتناهی و علم ذاتی و هستی جاودانی کرد: و **ذَلِكَ**

الْفَوْزُ الْعَظِيمُ (۸۹:۹)، استمداد[۳۱۶] این قوم باین صفات اقتضای عجز نامتناهی و جهل کلی و نیستی همیشگی کند: و **ذَٰلِكَ الْخِزْيُ الْعَظِيمُ** (۶۳:۹).

فصل هیجدهم
در اشارت به درخت طوبی و درخت زقوم

[§۸۳] علم و قدرت و ارادت که مبادی ایجاد افعال اند خلق را سه صفت مختلف است و خدای را هر سه یکی. اما به اعتبارات مختلف که نسبت با عقول خلق باشد، خلق را سه صفت نماید. وخود در ضمایر ما که نسبتی با عالم امر دارد [اگر] تصور صورتی معقول نامحسوس کنیم آن صورت از آن روی که تصور کرده ایم معلوم ما است و ما به آن عالم باشیم، و از آن روی که ایجادش کرده ایم مقدور ما باشد و ما بر آن قادر باشیم و از آن روی که ما تا نخواستیم متصور نشد مراد ما است و ما بدان مرید. پس معلوم و مقدور و مراد ما هر سه یکی است و در این صورت علم و قدرت و ارادت متحد شد. هم چنین جمله موجودات به نسبت با علم و قدرت و ارادت او تعالی همین حکم دارد. پس او را هر سه صفت متحد باشد بلکه واحد بود.

[§۸٤] و کسی که به علم او عالم باشد و به قدرت او قادر و به ارادتش مرید، چنانکه در حالت اهل بهشت گفتیم، و چنانکه <در خبر>[۳۱۷] آمده است: "کنت سمعه الذی یسمع به و بصره الذی یبصر به"[۳۱۸] حکمش همین بود: <"اطعنی اجعلک مثلی و لیس کمثله شیء و هو السمیع البصیر">[۳۱۹] پس هرچه ارادت او به آن تعلق گیرد هم در حال موجود شود، یعنی تمنی و وجدانش یکی باشد. و این معنی مثال درخت طوبی است در بهشت که هرچه بهشتیان آرزو کنند آرزوی ایشان دفعة واحدة بدان درخت حاصل باشد و در پیش ایشان حاضر: **طُوبَىٰ لَهُمْ وَحُسْنُ مَآبٍ** (۲۹:۱۳).

[§۸۵] و به ازاء این حال کسانی را که این سه صفت اقتضاء تکثر کند به حسب هر یکی نوعی از ناکامی و عذاب تولد کند: **انطَلِقُوا إِلَىٰ ظِلٍّ ذِي ثَلَاثِ شُعَبٍ. لَا ظَلِيلٍ وَلَا يُغْنِي مِنَ اللَّهَبِ** (۷۷:۳۱-۳۰). پس به جای درخت طوبی ایشان را درخت زقوم باشد: **إِنَّهَا شَجَرَةٌ تَخْرُجُ فِي أَصْلِ الْجَحِيمِ. طَلْعُهَا كَأَنَّهُ رُؤُوسُ الشَّيَاطِينِ** (۳۷:۶۵-۶۴). طلع ابتداء وجود تخم است که سبب انبات درخت باشد و رؤس[۳۲۰] الشیاطین <اهواء جزویه:>[۳۲۱] "إن الشیطان لتجری من ابن آدم مجری الدم فی العروق."[۳۲۲] و رؤس ایشان [که] مبادی <اهوای انفس>[۳۲۳] باشد طلع این درخت است و منشأ هاویه.

فصل نوزدهم
در اشارت به حور عين

[§۸۶] چون دیده بصیرت مرد به کُحْل توفیق گشاده شود <و ابراهیم وار بر مطالعه ملکوت هر دو کون قادر شود:>[۳۲۴] **وَكَذَٰلِكَ نُرِي إِبْرَاهِيمَ مَلَكُوتَ السَّمَاوَاتِ وَالْأَرْضِ وَلِيَكُونَ مِنَ الْمُوقِنِينَ** (۶:۷۵)، واردان حضرت عزت که از پرده غیب ظهور میکنند در یک یک ذرات کائنات خویشتن را بواسطهء نورِ تجلی جلوه میدهند مشاهده و لامحاله چنانکه گفته اند هریک در نیکوترین صورتی از صورِ مخلوقات متمثل شوند. مانند آنکه در قصه مریم آمده است: **فَتَمَثَّلَ لَهَا بَشَرًا سَوِيًّا** (۱۹:۱۷).

[§۸۷] و چون تمتع از آن مشاهده جز به فیضان اثری از عالم وحدت که مقتضی ازدواج ذات و صورت باشد با یکدیگر بر وجهی که مفضی به اتحاد بود صورت نه بندد، پس با هر یکی از آن صور که به منزله[۳۲۵] یکی از حوران بهشت باشند[۳۲۶] این ازدواج حاصل گردد: **وَزَوَّجْنَاهُم بِحُورٍ عِينٍ**(۴۴:۵۴). و بدان سبب که چهرهء آن حوران از دیده اغیار [و] اهل تضاد مصون است: **حُورٌ مَّقْصُورَاتٌ فِي الْخِيَامِ** (۵۵:۷۲)، و به حکم آنکه نامحرمان عالم تکثر را، چه آن قوم را که به ظاهر عالم ملک

بازمانده اند و چه آن قوم را که به باطن عالم ملکوت محجوب شده اند، وصل ایشان نا ممکن است: **لَمْ يَطْمِثْهُنَّ إِنسٌ قَبْلَهُمْ وَلَا جَانٌّ** (۷۴:۵۵). و به سبب آنکه معاودت آن حالت هر نوبت التذاذی زیادت از نوبت اول باشد، هم چون مفقودی که بعد از مقاسات طلب مفاوضه باز یافته شود، بکارت و عزابت آن لذت هر نوبت متجدد شود.

فصل بیستم
در اشارت به ثواب و عقاب وعدل او

[§۸۸] ثواب از فضل خداست و عقاب از عدل او. بدین سبب گفت: **مَن جَاء بِالْحَسَنَةِ فَلَهُ خَيْرٌ مِّنْهَا وَمَن جَاء بِالسَّيِّئَةِ فَلَا يُجْزَى الَّذِينَ عَمِلُوا السَّيِّئَاتِ إِلَّا مَا كَانُوا يَعْمَلُونَ** (۸۴:۲۸). و هم چنین: **مَن جَاء بِالْحَسَنَةِ فَلَهُ عَشْرُ أَمْثَالِهَا وَمَن جَاء بِالسَّيِّئَةِ فَلاَ يُجْزَى إِلاَّ مِثْلَهَا** (۱۶۰:۶). و در موضعی دیگر: **مَّثَلُ الَّذِينَ يُنفِقُونَ أَمْوَالَهُمْ فِي سَبِيلِ اللّهِ كَمَثَلِ حَبَّةٍ أَنبَتَتْ سَبْعَ سَنَابِلَ فِي كُلِّ سُنبُلَةٍ مِّئَةُ حَبَّةٍ وَاللّهُ يُضَاعِفُ لِمَن يَشَاء** (۲۶۱:۲).

[§۸۹] اما قومی هستند که از حیّز فضل اند: **يُبَدِّلُ اللَّهُ سَيِّئَاتِهِمْ حَسَنَاتٍ** (۷۰:۲۵) و به ازاء ایشان آنها که **حَبِطَتْ أَعْمَالُهُمْ** (۲۱۷:۲)؛ وقومی هستند که از حیّز عدل اند: **فَمَن يَعْمَلْ مِثْقَالَ ذَرَّةٍ خَيْرًا يَرَهُ. وَمَن**

يَعْمَلْ مِثْقَالَ ذَرَّةٍ شَرًّا يَرَهُ (۹۹:۸-۷). و به ازاء ایشان آنها که **لاَ جَرَمَ أَنَّهُمْ فِي الآخِرَةِ هُمُ الأَخْسَرُونَ** (۱۱:۲۲).[۳۲۷]

[§۹۰] و هم چنین قومی: **يُؤْتِكُمْ كِفْلَيْنِ مِن رَّحْمَتِهِ** (۵۷:۲۸)، و قومی را: **سَنُعَذِّبُهُم مَّرَّتَيْنِ** (۹:۱۰۱). وقومی را در ثواب: **يُضَاعَفُ لَهُمْ وَلَهُمْ أَجْرٌ كَرِيمٌ** (۵۷:۱۸) وقومی را: **يُضَاعَفُ لَهُمُ الْعَذَابُ** (۱۱:۲۰) و این تفاوت به سبب تفاوتی است که در سیئات و حسنات باشد نسبت با هر قومی، که "حسنات الابرار سیأت المقربین." و از سیئه آدم تا سیئه ابلیس تفاوت بسیار است. در خبر است که "ضربة علی یوم الخندق توازی عمل الثقلین."

[§۹۱] پس بالای همه ثوابها ثواب کسانی است که بحکم آن جهان خودی خود در بازند: "وفوق کل بِرّ بر حتی یقتل الرجل فی سبیل الله." هم چنانکه بالای همه عِقابها عِقابی است که به حکم این جهان خودی خود دریابند: **الَّذِينَ خَسِرُواْ أَنفُسَهُمْ** (۶:۱۲).

[§۹۲] آنها که اعمال ایشان با ثواب متحد است اهل فوز اکبر اند: **فَلَا تَعْلَمُ نَفْسٌ مَّا أُخْفِيَ لَهُم مِّن قُرَّةِ أَعْيُنٍ** (۳۲:۱۷)، ایشان راست: "مالا عین رأت ولا اذن سمعت ولا خطر علی قلب بشر."[۳۲۸] ایشان از ثواب و

عقاب منزه اند، چه دنیا وآخرت بر مرد خدا حرام است: "الدنیا حرام علی اهل الآخرة والآخرة حرام علی اهل الدنیا و هما حرامان علی اهل الله." [۳۲۹]

[§۹۳] اینست آن چه تحریرش در این وقت دست داد. انتظار به بینندگان که در این فصلها نظر کنند آنست دعای خیر دریغ ندارند و اصلاح سهو ها که قابل اصلاح باشد بجای آرند.[۳۳۰] <والله اعلم واحکم و حسبنا الله ونعم الوکیل.

[§۹۴] تم الکتاب بعون الملک الوهاب عصیره یوم الأحد، النیروز الجلالی فی خاسر ربیع الاول، ثالث شهور سنه ثلاث و عشرین و سبعمائه. حرره صاحبه الفقیر الی الله الودود الحاج ابو محمد، محمد بن ابی الفتح مسعود. رب اغفر له.> [۳۳۱]

اختلافات نسخ

۱. تولا و تبرا:

[۱] اضافات و تصحیحات قیاسی از استاد فقید محمد تقی دانش پژوه مصحح متن تولا وتبرا میباشد. [۲] در متن "محقق" که ظاهراً غلط است. بنگرید به روضه تسلیم یا تصورات [۴۷۸§] و سیر وسلوک[۴۴§]. [۳] در متن: بخردی.

۲. **مطلوب المؤمنین:** علائم اختصاری: 'ق' قدیمی ترین نسخه موجود در مؤسسه مطالعات اسماعیلی، لندن؛ نخ: سایر نسخ متأخر که در مقدمه انگلیسی به آنها اشاره شده است.

[۱] نخ + که این. [۲] نخ: قابل. [۳] نخ: داند. [۴] باستثنای مواردی که در پانوشت به آنها اشاره شده، مطالب داخل کروشه فقط در نسخه 'ق' موجود است. [۵] نخ: لایزال [۶] 'ق' : اهل. [۷] نخ: معاملات. [۸] نخ + این بنده گسیل این چند. [۹] نخ + تا کسانیکه طالب دین حق باشند پیروی نمایند. [۱۰] نخ+ واین حقیر. [۱۱]. نخ: مخادمان. [۱۲] نخ: چون این رساله را ملاحظه نمایند. [۱۳] نخ: دارند. [۱۴] نخ: وجود. [۱۵] نخ: ذکرهم السلام. [۱۶] نخ: فرمایند. [۱۷] نخ: فهرست فصل های مطلوب المؤمنین که به تفصیل می آید این است. [۱۸] نخ: مرد. [۱۹] نخ: اثر. [۲۰] نخ+ بوده. [۲۱] بنگرید به پانوشت۶۲ ذیل این حدیث در ترجمه انگلیسی. [۲۲] نخ+ مقصود آفرینش این عالم او بود. [۲۳] نخ+ هر آدم عاقل را. [۲۴] نخ+ بجای آورد و. [۲۵] نخ: که. [۲۶] نخ+ بداند و. [۲۷] نخ+ به معرفت. [۲۸] نخ: فرزندان بحق. [۲۹] نخ+ ومن مات ولم یعرف إمام زمانه فمات میته جاهلیه و الجاهل فی النار. یعنی هرکس بمیرد و امام زمان خود را نشناسد مرگ او مرگ جاهلان باشد. [۳۰] نخ + یعنی نیافریدم پری و آدمی را إلا از بهر آنکه مرا بپرستند و بشناسند و عبادت کنند. [۳۱] 'ق': ندارد. [۳۲] 'ق': ندارد. [۳۳] 'ق': ندارد. [۳۴] نخ+ افتاده باشد. [۳۵] نخ + امر و.

[۳۶] نخ: است همه را. [۳۷] نخ + چنانچه از امر واجب الوجود موجود شده است. [۳۸] نخ + قوله تعالی. [۳۹] نخ + باز گردد به اصل خود همه چیز - زر صافی و نقره و ارزیز. [۴۰] نخ: مؤمنی. [۴۱] نخ + به اثبات حجت اعظم. [۴۲] نخ+ و فرمان. [۴۳] نخ+ چون جان و. [۴۴] نخ+ که همه عاریت است. [۴۵] 'ق': ندارد. [۴۶] نخ+ قوله تعالی. [۴۷] 'ق' : داشتن. [۴۸] نخ: یعنی ذات و حقیقت را به یقین دانستن. [۴۹] 'ق' : ندارد. [۵۰] 'ق': بطلبند. [۵۱] نخ+ هر دو. [۵۲] نخ+ رسول علیه السلام فرمودند که دنیا حرام است بر اهل آخرت وآخرت حرام است بر اهل دنیا و هر دو حرام است بر اهل الله تعالی. [۵۳] نخ+ بجود ولی الزمان. [۵۴] نخ+ هریک. [۵۵] نخ: امر. [۵۶] نخ: جز اوست ببرند و بیزارشوند. [۵۷] نخ + واین چهار چیز. [۵۸] 'ق': ندارد. [۵۹] نخ + بپرستند [۶۰] 'ق': ندارد. [۶۱] نخ + که همه عاریت است. [۶۲] نخ + و بیزار شوند. [۶۳] نخ + وجهاد کنند. [۶۴] نخ + حقیقی که یاد کرده شد بجود ولی زمان. [۶۵] 'ق': ندارد. [۶۶] نخ: دانش. [۶۷] نخ + آن را بداند که باطن است. [۶۸] 'ق' + آن. [۶۹] نخ + و رسول خدا. [۷۰] نخ: گردانی. [۷۱] در 'ق' بجای آیه(۷۰:۲۳) حدیث ... وحافظوا السنتکم و ابصارکم ولا تحاسدوا ولا تنازعوا و لا تباغضوا ولا تنابزو... درج شده است. [۷۲] نخ+ ده یک بیت المال امام زمان برسانی یا آنکه به فرمان مولانا. [۷۳] نخ+ و او را بکشی، فرد: نفس مردود است او را رد کنید، پس مکان بر عالم سرمد کنید. [۷۴] نخ: باقی. [۷۵] 'ق': ندارد. [۷۶] نخ: ندارد. [۷۷] نخ + یا صاحب العصر و الزمان، آمین یا رب لعالمین برحمتک یا ارحم الراحمین. تمام شد رساله ی مطلوب المؤمنین به تاریخ پانزده صفر المظفر سنه ی ۱۳۵۲.

۳. **آغاز و انجام:** علائم اختصاری: س: سفینه تبریز؛ ت: نسخه تهران چاپ ایرج افشار؛ ب: نسخه کتابخانه بادلیان اکسفورد؛ م؛ نسخه کتابخانه دانشکده ادبیات دانشگاه مشهد.

[۱] س + کتاب آغاز و انجام از تصنیف مولانا معظم سعید مغفور افضل المتأخرین نصیرالمله والدین الطوسی طاب ثراه. [۲] ت، م،ب+ او. [۳] ت، م: پیغمبرانی [۴] س + وآلش علیه السلام و رضی الله عنهم. [۵] ت: بر محمد النبی صلی الله علیه، ب: بر محمد و آل طیبین او. [۶] ت: دوستی از عزیزان. [۷] فقط در: ب. [۸] فقط در: ب. [۹] س: کنند. [۱۰] ب: آغاز و انجام آفرینش. [۱۱] ت، ب: خدای تعالی، م: خدا. [۱۲] س: علیه السلام و رضی الله عنهم. [۱۳] ب + بعث. [۱۴] ب: کن. [۱۵] ت م ب: کرده اند. [۱۶] فقط در: س و ب. [۱۷] ت: ندارد. [۱۸] ت م: کسی. [۱۹] ت: نبشت. [۲۰] س: ندارد. [۲۱] فقط در ت، سایر نسخ: ملتفت. [۲۲] ت م: نداشت، س: نداند. [۲۳] س: ندارد. [۲۴] ت م: باشد. [۲۵] س + ان شاء الله. [۲۶] س و ب : ندارد. [۲۷] ب: الاخیار. [۲۸] ب: ندارد. [۲۹] ب: ندارد. [۳۰] ب: فهرست مندرجات را ندارد. [۳۱] ت+ در جهان. [۳۲] س، م: ندارد. [۳۳] ت: و در این دقیقه. [۳۴] در تمام نسخ: حالش. [۳۵] ب: ندارد. [۳۶] س: رئوس. [۳۷] ت: اول. [۳۸] ب: ندارد. [۳۹] ب: تخیلات. [۴۰]

ت: ناخوانا است. [۴۱] ب: مطاوعت. [۴۲]س: آسا. [۴۳] ب: ندارد. [۴۴] س: ندارد، ت: تنگی.[۴۵] ب: بالاتر از آنکه. [۴۶] ب: باشد. [۴۷] س: ندارد. [۴۸] ب: سریست. [۴۹] ت: ندارد. [۵۰] س: بانجام، ب: بدینجا، ت: بانجام. [۵۱] س: اول. [۵۲] س م ب: باول. . [۵۳] م: از این سبب. [۵۴] ب: ندارد. [۵۵] س: هریکی عکس دیگر، ب: هریک عکس یکدیگر، م: ناخوانا است. [۵۶] م: نبوده هست شده اند، ت: ونبوده اند پس بآخر هست شده اند. [۵۷] س و م: بهشت. [۵۸] م: معاد موجود باشد آنجاست. [۵۹] م و ت: ندارد. [۶۰] م و ت: ندارد [۶۱] م: ندارد. [۶۲] ب: اول افول و نزول دوم طلوع. [۶۳] س: ندارد. [۶۴] س: ندارد. [۶۵] س: ندارد. [۶۶] س: ندارد. [۶۷] م: ندارد. [۶۸] س: ندارد. [۶۹] بنگرید به پانوشت۷۳ ذیل همین حدیث در بخش انگلیسی. [۷۰] بنگرید به پانوشت۷۴ ذیل همین حدیث در بخش انگلیسی. [۷۱] س: ندارد. [۷۲] ت: موقع. [۷۳] س + و ما کتب الی اول. [۷۴] ت: مراد. [۷۵] ت+ صلی الله علیه و آله، ب + مصطفی علیه السلام. [۷۶] ب: ندارد. [۷۷] بنگرید به پانوشت ۷۵ ذیل همین حدیث در بخش انگلیسی. [۷۸] ت+ صلی الله علیه و آله. [۷۹] بنگرید به پانوشت ذیل همین حدیث در بخش انگلیسی. [۸۰] ت + مصطفی صلی لله علیه وآله. [۸۱] بنگرید به پانوشت۷۷ ذیل همین حدیث در بخش انگلیسی. [۸۲] متن این پاراگراف در ت، ب و م مقدم مؤخر است. [۸۳] ت،م: شهادت به غیب. بنگرید به فصل پنجم. با توجه به این نکته که دنیا عالم ایمان به غیب و آخرت است وایقان به آنچه در آخرت مشاهده میشود پس انسان از عالم غیب و پوشیدگي ها به شهادت و از عالم مشابهت به عالم مباینت سفر میکند. [۸۴] س:

انبیا. [۸۵] س: برازخ. [۸۶] س،ت: الناس حلم [۸۷] بنگرید به پانوشت۷۹ ذیل همین حدیث در بخش انگلیسی. [۸۸] س، م: ولکن. [۸۹] ب: ندارد. [۹۰] بنگرید به پانوشت۸۰ ذیل همین حدیث در بخش انگلیسی. [۹۱] ب + و برخاسته. [۹۲] بنگرید به پانوشت۸۱ ذیل همین عبارت در بخش انگلیسی. [۹۳] ب + و هنوز متنبه نشده باشد. [۹۴] ب: هلاکت جاودانی افتاد.. [۹۵] س: کشف آن، م، ت: کشف آن سر. [۹۶] ب + مصطفی صلی الله علیه و آله. م: محمد که. [۹۷] ت، م + که. [۹۸] بنگرید به پانوشت۸۳ ذیل همین حدیث در بخش انگلیسی. [۹۹] س: ندارد. [۱۰۰] س: مقام آن. [۱۰۱] ب + حکم. [۱۰۲] س: ندارد. [۱۰۳] ب، م: ندارد. [۱۰۴] س: سالکان. [۱۰۵] ب: چه. [۱۰۶] س: ندارد. [۱۰۷] س + در. [۱۰۸] س: ندارد. [۱۰۹] س: ندارد. [۱۱۰] س: ندارد. [۱۱۱] س: چه. [۱۱۲] س: علم توجه این جهانیست و مشاهده روئیت آن جهانست. [۱۱۳] س: ندارد. [۱۱۴] س: اتقان. [۱۱۵] س: ندارد. [۱۱۶] س + نخست. [۱۱۷] س + نخست. [۱۱۸] ب، م، ت: اقبل. [۱۱۹] بنگرید به پانوشت۸۶ ذیل همین عبارت در بخش انگلیسی. [۱۲۰] س: اتقان. [۱۲۱] س: ندارد. [۱۲۲] ب: ندارد. [۱۲۳] س: وصول. [۱۲۴] م: عین. [۱۲۵] ب. پل. [۱۲۶] س: بعد از سوال از آن. [۱۲۷] عبارت در م، ت: مشاهده دوزخ بعد از حصول علم الیقین است و مشاهده بهشت قبل از سوال. از آنکه هنوز [علم م: ندارد] حکم غیب دارد و بعد از حصول علم عین الیقین است چه با علم هنوز حجاب باقیست بعین و با عین باقیست باثر. [۱۲۸] س: نفس. [۱۲۹] ب + و هم مکان. [۱۳۰] ب: ندارد. [۱۳۱] ب: کمال.

[۱۳۲] م: صلی الله علیه و آله. [۱۳۳] ب: دراز. [۱۳۴] ب: تا حارثه مشاهده آن حال کرد برای آنکه او مؤمن حقیقی است. [۱۳۵] بنگرید به پانوشت۸۹ ذیل همین حدیث در بخش انگلیسی. [۱۳۶] س، ب وم: ندارد. [۱۳۷] س: طفل او را، ت: طفل را، ب: کودک خورد که او را. [۱۳۸] م: ندارد. [۱۳۹] س: احاطت بکائنات. [۱۴۰] ت: این احاطه. [۱۴۱] س ب + و اثرش غیر او را. [۱۴۲] ب: ندارد. [۱۴۳] س: شد. [۱۴۴] س + خود. [۱۴۵] س : ندارد، ب: هم تمام. [۱۴۶] س + چون. [۱۴۷] م: جوهر. [۱۴۸] م + می کند. [۱۴۹] س + است. [۱۵۰] م: ندارد. [۱۵۱] س: ندارد. [۱۵۲] س: ندارد. [۱۵۳] س: ندارد. [۱۵۴] س ب م: الیقین خطرات. [۱۵۵] م: پس. [۱۵۶] س، ب: ندارد. [۱۵۷] س: حکومه. [۱۵۸] م + که در برابر یکدیگر نشسته اند. [۱۵۹] س: ندارد. [۱۶۰] س: ب: ندارد. [۱۶۱] س، م: ندارد. [۱۶۲] م: بآن است. [۱۶۳] س: واحشر مع من یتقی الله، ت: واحشره مع من کان یتولاه.[۱۶۴] م: الحسن و یحشر عندها. [۱۶۵] س، م: واینجا هم کسانی اند که اهل این جهان باشند، ت: ولکن در این جهان کسانی بینندة اهل آن جهان را باشند. [۱۶۶] م ت ب: ذکر. [۱۶۷] م: ندارد. [۱۶۸] م: سالکان راه وحدت اند که. [۱۶۹] س: این. [۱۷۰] م: بندگان. [۱۷۱] م: ندارد. [۱۷۲] م: ندارد. [۱۷۳] ب: ندارد. [۱۷۴] س: ندارد. [۱۷۵] ب: سابقان واهل یمین در بهشت باشند. [۱۷۶] س + بهشت ببهشت باشد. [۱۷۷] م: اهل یمین بهشت سابقان. [۱۷۸] بنگرید به پانوشت۹۶ ذیل همین حدیث در بخش انگلیسی. [۱۷۹] م: ندارد. [۱۸۰] س، م: ندارد. [۱۸۱] م: ندارد. [۱۸۲] ب: ندارد. [۱۸۳] ب: بمانده. [۱۸۴] ب. ندارد. [۱۸۵] س + خالدین. [۱۸۶] ب: در.

[۱۸۷] س: اگر. [۱۸۸] س: ندارد. [۱۸۹] م: ندارد. [۱۹۰] س: ندارد. [۱۹۱] م: عبارت مقدم ومؤخر است. [۱۹۲] ب: ندارد. [۱۹۳] س: سبب. [۱۹۴] م + الظانین بالله سؤالظن. [۱۹۵] م +گاه سبب. [۱۹۶] س + است. [۱۹۷] س: ندارد. [۱۹۸] م: نسبت. [۱۹۹] س: ندارد. [۲۰۰] م: از، ب: که از. [۲۰۱] ت م + اهل. [۲۰۲] م: شمال عن شمالهم یسارهم. [۲۰۳] ب: یسار. [۲۰۴] ب: کلتا بینی الرحمن یمین، ت: کلتا یدی الرحمن، م: کلما یدی الرحمن یمین. [۲۰۵] س: ندارد. [۲۰۶] س، ب: باشد؛ م: بوند. [۲۰۷] س: هر فکری یا قولی بکند اثری از آن او با او باقی بماند؛ م: اثری از او با او. [۲۰۸] ت: معادات. [۲۰۹] ب: شود و باشد. [۲۱۰] س: ندارد. [۲۱۱] ب: ندارد. [۲۱۲] ب: احوال؛ م: کتاب صحیفه اعمال. [۲۱۳] م: متشخص. [۲۱۴] س: وحده؛ م: ندارد. [۲۱۵] م: آنان. [۲۱۶] ب: ندارد. [۲۱۷] ب + همچنین. [۲۱۸] ب: هم اینجاست. [۲۱۹] ب: ملک؛ م + شیطان. [۲۲۰] ب: ملکه. [۲۲۱] س ب ت: ندارد. [۲۲۲] س؛ م: ندارد. [۲۲۳] س؛ م: یدخل. [۲۲۴] س: ندارد. [۲۲۵] ب؛ م + همچنین. [۲۲۶] س + بسیار. [۲۲۷] ب: آنکس که. [۲۲۸] س + مثلا. [۲۲۹] س: ندارد. [۲۳۰] س: این. [۲۳۱] پایان فصل هفتم در نسخه ب. [۲۳۲] بنگرید به پانوشت۱۰۷ ذیل همین حدیث در بخش انگلیسی. [۲۳۳] س: ندارد. [۲۳۴] بنگرید به پانوشت۱۰۸ ذیل همین حدیث در بخش انگلیسی. [۲۳۵] م ت ب: ندارد. [۲۳۶] س: ندارد. [۲۳۷] س: منکوسانی باشد که. [۲۳۸] ب: ندارد. [۲۳۹] ب+ اند که. [۲۴۰] ب: طایفه. [۲۴۱] ب: تا. [۲۴۲] س: ندارد. [۲۴۳] م +کرده. [۲۴۴] ب + صلی الله علیه و آله. [۲۴۵] به قرینه متن

افزوده شد. [۲۴۶] س: حسنات. [۲۴۷] ب: که یبدل الله سیئاتهم حسنات. [۲۴۸] بنگرید به پانوشت۱۱۱ ذیل همین حدیث در بخش انگلیسی. [۲۴۹] بنگرید به پانوشت۱۱۲ ذیل همین حدیث در بخش انگلیسی. س: عذب. [۲۵۰] بنگرید به پانوشت۱۱۳ ذیل همین حدیث در بخش انگلیسی. [۲۵۱] س: ندارد. [۲۵۲] م: نکند. [۲۵۳] م: اثر. [۲۵۴] س: بحقیقت باید. [۲۵۵] س، م: ندارد. [۲۵۶] س: و از اختلاف. [۲۵۷] بنگرید به پانوشت۱۱۴ ذیل همین حدیث در بخش انگلیسی. [۲۵۸] س: ندارد، ب: اثر آنچه نفس را مانع هواهای مختلف کند و اثر نفس و تتبع هواهای مختلف کند معنیش بحقیقت اولی. [۲۵۹] ب، م: ندارد. [۲۶۰] بنگرید به پانوشت۱۱۵ ذیل همین حدیث در بخش انگلیسی. [۲۶۱] ت: ترتبی. [۲۶۲] ت: متشخص. [۲۶۳] ت: هم چنانکه.[۲۶۴] س+ اعمال.[۲۶۵] ب: عز و جل. [۲۶۶] س، م، ت: و. [۲۶۷] س: آن. [۲۶۸] س: ندارد. [۲۶۹] ت+ میگویند و. [۲۷۰] ت: گفته شد. [۲۷۱] ب: کند. [۲۷۲] س: تعویلی. [۲۷۳] ت: عواد مقالات و نشر اداء دیانات؛ ب: عوار مقالات و کسر آراء دیانات. [۲۷۴] س: ندلرد. [۲۷۵] بنگرید به پانوشت۱۱۸ ذیل همین حدیث در بخش انگلیسی. [۲۷۶] بنگرید به پانوشت۱۱۹ ذیل همین حدیث در بخش انگلیسی. [۲۷۷] م: ندارد. [۲۷۸] م: تشبیه ها و برار. [۲۷۹] ب: ندارد. [۲۸۰] م: ندارد. [۲۸۱] س: ندارد. [۲۸۲] م: ندارد. [۲۸۳] ت، به نقل از چاپ های مقدم و م + فی تفسیر قوله تعالی، روی عن الصادق علیه السلام: وجیء یومئذ بجهنم إذا کان یوم القیمه یناد جهنم علی صوره جمل بسبعین الف زمام فی ید سبعین الف ملک الی أن یطلع علیها الخلایق فشرده شرده لولا أن حبسها الله لأحترقت السموات وألأرض. نیز بنگرید به پانوشت ۱۲۰ ذیل همین حدیث در بخش

انگلیسی. [۲۸۴] م: خمس. [۲۸۵] س: صورت. [۲۸۶] س،م، ب: ندارد. [۲۸۷] س: مشاعر. [۲۸۸] ت: خلقی. [۲۸۹] ت، م: برج. ب: میدان دوازده برج. [۲۹۰] فقط در: ب. [۲۹۱] فقط در: ب. [۲۹۲] فقط در: ب. [۲۹۳] س. محرک. [۲۹۴] س: گذرد. [۲۹۵] بنگرید به پانوشت۱۲۳ ذیل همین حدیث در بخش انگلیسی. [۲۹۶] ب: ندارد. [۲۹۷] س: ندارد. [۲۹۸] ب: ظاهر [۲۹۹] . ب: ندارد. [۳۰۰] س: ندارد. [۳۰۱] س: ندارد. [۳۰۲] ب: ندارد. [۳۰۳] س: ندارد. [۳۰۴] ت، م + که در نشأه اولی بوده است؛ ب + در نشأت. [۳۰۵] س، م: ندارد. [۳۰۶] س: ندارد. [۳۰۷] س، م، ت: بطش. [۳۰۸] ب + قوتها. [۳۰۹] س: موجب. [۳۱۰] ت+ کل. [۳۱۱] ب: مراد. [۳۱۲] ب: نبود [۳۱۳] ب: همگی. [۳۱۴] ب: ندارد. [۳۱۵] س: انتفاع. [۳۱۶] ت: استعداد. [۳۱۷] س: ندارد. [۳۱۸] بنگرید به پانوشت۱۲۷ ذیل همین حدیث در بخش انگلیسی[۳۱۹] س: ندارد. [۳۲۰] س: ندارد. [۳۲۱] ب: امراء موذیه؛ ت: اهواء مردیه؛ م: اهواء. [۳۲۲] بنگرید به پانوشت۱۳۰ ذیل همین حدیث در بخش انگلیسی. [۳۲۳] س: اشخاص. [۳۲۴] س:ندارد. [۳۲۵] س: مراتب. [۳۲۶] س: هاست. [۳۲۷] ت+ در شأن ایشان است. [۳۲۸] بنگرید به پانوشت۱۳۴ ذیل همین حدیث در بخش انگلیسی. [۳۲۹] بنگرید به پانوشت۱۳۵ ذیل همین حدیث در بخش انگلیسی. [۳۳۰] پایان نسخه ب؛ م با عبارت : سبحان ربک رب العزه عما یصفون و سلام علی المرسلین والحمد لله رب العالمین. اللهم اغفر لی و لوالدی و جمیع المؤمنین والمؤمنات بحق محمد وآله اجمعین. فرغت من تتمیمه چهارشنبه شهر

جمادی الاول من سنه ثلاث و ثمانین و الف بعد الهجره علی صاحبها بعدد علم الله الصلواه و التحیات [امضا ناخوانا]. و، ت با عبارت: الله ولی التوفیق سبحان ربک رب العزه عما یصفون و سلام علی المرسلین والحمد لله رب العالمین به پایان میرسد. [۳۳۱] م، ت، ب: ندارد.

Persian Texts